Eureka!

Eureka!

VOLUME 2: C-E

Edited by
Linda Schmittroth,
Mary Reilly McCall
& Bridget Travers

AN IMPRINT OF GALE RESEARCH INC.,
AN INTERNATIONAL THOMPSON PUBLISHING COMPANY

Changing the Way the World Learns

NEW YORK • LONDON • BONN • BOSTON • DETROIT • MADRID
MELBOURNE • MEXICO CITY • PARIS • SINGAPORE • TOKYO
TORONTO • WASHINGTON • ALBANY NY • BELMONT CA • CINCINNATI OH

Eureka!

Scientific Discoveries and Inventions That Shaped the World

Edited by **Linda Schmittroth, Mary Reilly McCall, and Bridget Travers**

Staff

Carol DeKane Nagel, *Developmental Editor*
Jane Hoehner, *Contributing Editor*
Julie L. Carnagie, *Assistant Editor*
Thomas L. Romig, *U·X·L Publisher*

Shanna P. Heilveil, *Production Associate*
Evi Seoud, *Assistant Production Manager*
Mary Beth Trimper, *Production Director*

Margaret A. Chamberlain, *Permissions Associate (Pictures)*

Pamela A. E. Galbreath, *Cover and Page Designer*
Cynthia Baldwin, *Art Director*

∞™ This book is printed on acid-free paper that meets the minimum requirements of American National Standard for Information Sciences—Permanence Paper for Printed Library Materials, ANSI Z39.48-1984.

ISBN: 0-8103-9802-8 (Set)
ISBN: 0-8103-9803-6 (Volume 1)
ISBN: 0-8103-9804-4 (Volume 2)
ISBN: 0-8103-9805-2 (Volume 3)
ISBN: 0-8103-9806-0 (Volume 4)
ISBN: 0-8103-9807-9 (Volume 5)
ISBN: 0-8103-9808-7 (Volume 6)

Printed in the United States of America

I(T)P™

U·X·L is an imprint of Gale Research,
an International Thomson Publishing Company.

ITP logo is a trademark under license.

Table of Contents

Reader's Guide

Eureka! Scientific Discoveries and Inventions That Shaped the World features 600 entries on scientific inventions and discoveries that have made a great impact on the world—from the principle of buoyancy to the atomic bomb, from blood transfusion to microcomputers—and the people responsible for them. Written in nontechnical language, *Eureka!* explores such important inventions as the ancient craft of brick-making, but focuses primarily on significant breakthroughs from the Industrial Revolution to the present day, including the invention of the steam engine and the discoveries made possible by the Hubble Space Telescope.

Each *Eureka!* entry, whether on a well-known discovery or a lesser-known invention, identifies the person behind the breakthrough, the knowledge and technology that led to it, and how these advances changed the world in which we live.

Scope and Format

Eureka!'s 600 entries are arranged alphabetically over six volumes. Entries range from one-quarter to eight pages and often include sidebar boxes discussing important breakthroughs, such as firsts in space flight, and lesser-known facts, such as how a frog helped invent the electric battery. Boldfaced terms in the text direct the reader to related entries in the set, while cross-references at the ends of entries alert the reader to related entries not specifically mentioned in that entry. More than 430 photographs and original illustrations enliven and help explain the text.

Each *Eureka!* volume begins with a listing of the featured discoveries and inventions arranged by 37 scientific categories. This handy category listing lets users quickly identify and locate related discoveries and inventions. The comprehensive general index found at the end of each volume provides easy access to the people, theories, and discoveries and inventions mentioned throughout *Eureka!*

Special Thanks and Dedication

The editors dedicate this work to their husbands and to their daughters, Margie and Sara, along with all the children of St. Agatha School in Redford, Michigan, and Bingham Farms Elementary School in Bingham Farms, Michigan. They would also like to express their sincere appreciation to teacher Marlene Heitmanis and tutor and counselor Theresa McCall for their guidance on school curricula.

Comments and Suggestions

We welcome your comments on this work as well as your suggestions for topics to be featured in future editions of *Eureka! Scientific Discoveries and Inventions That Shaped the World*. Please write: Editors, *Eureka!* U·X·L, 835 Penobscot Bldg., Detroit, Michigan 48226-4094; call toll-free: 1-800-877-4253; or fax 1-313-877-6348.

Inventions and Discoveries by Subject

Bold numerals indicate volume numbers.

Civil engineering and construction

Clothing and textiles and their manufacture

**I n v e n t i o n s
a n d
D i s c o v e r i e s
b y S u b j e c t**

Electronics

Environmental sciences/ecology

Everyday items

Food/food science

Geology

Metallurgy

Meteorology

Musical instruments

Security systems and related items

Sports, games, toys, and fads

Timepieces, measuring devices, and related items

Transportation

Weapons and related items

Picture Credits

The photographs appearing in *Eureka! Scientific Discoveries and Inventions That Shaped the World* were received from the following sources:

©**Bernard Uhlig/Phototake NYC:** p. 9; ©**Yoav Levy/Phototake NYC:** pp. 16, 392, 549, 806, 819, 931; ©**Tony Freeman/Photo Edit:** pp. 18, 325, 380, 462, 543, 562, 638; **AP/Wide World Photos:** pp. 21, 30, 35, 67, 68, 78, 124, 139, 141, 151, 164, 257, 261, 266, 285, 294, 298, 314, 332, 365, 373, 374, 465, 495, 516, 523, 578, 580, 672, 676, 679, 695, 696, 714, 731, 747, 748, 749, 823, 830, 833, 850, 852, 854, 865, 866, 888, 902, 910, 917, 930, 938, 945, 984, 994, 1002, 1008, 1020, 1034, 1044, 1047, 1057, 1059, 1061, 1079, 1090, 1093, 1153, 1172; **UPI/Bettmann:** pp. 26, 32, 51, 79, 90, 137, 148, 159, 235, 272, 287, 289, 364, 450, 458, 477, 490, 504, 546, 558, 559, 599, 634, 681, 689, 699, 710, 727, 807, 811, 849, 871, 901, 905, 911, 934, 1027, 1029, 1046, 1077, 1150, 1176; **Reuters/Bettmann:** pp. 37, 81, 601, 878, 916; **Bettmann Archive:** pp. 42, 43, 121, 122, 145, 157, 174, 180, 185, 228, 244, 253, 401, 411, 445, 484, 489, 533, 566, 582, 677, 690, 716, 733, 813, 816, 831, 832, 839, 862, 867, 875, 876, 882, 913, 919, 939, 948, 983, 989, 1016, 1018, 1038, 1042, 1053, 1063, 1102, 1136, 1167; ©**Michael Newman/Photo Edit:** pp. 49, 448, 853, 1096; ©**The Telegraph Colour Library/FPG International:** pp. 59, 100, 226, 320, 598; ©**Anna E. Zuckerman/Photo Edit:** p. 64; ©**Jon Gordon/Phototake NYC:** p. 65; ©**Kent Knudson/FPG International:** p. 76; ©**Martin Roiker/Phototake NYC:** p. 82; ©**Account Phototake/Phototake NYC:** pp. 85, 108, 501, 742; ©**Howard Sochurek 1986/The Stock Market:** p. 87; **Dar al-Athar al-Islamiyyah, Ministry of Information, Kuwait:** p. 97; **Courtesy of the Department of Energy:** p. 119; ©**1992 Howard Sochurek/The Stock Market:** p. 129; ©**Dr. Den-**

nis Kunkel/Phototake NYC: pp. 130, 260, 1039; ©David Young-Wolff/Photo Edit: pp. 136, 378, 449; The Science Museum/Science & Society Picture Library: pp. 143, 274; ©1976 Isaiah Karlinsky/FPG International: p. 163; ©Goivaux Communication/Phototake NYC: p. 165; ©1988 David Frazier/The Stock Market: p. 172; ©1986 Randy Duchaine/The Stock Market: p. 178; ©Hammond Incorporated, Maplewood, New Jersey, License #12, 231: 187; ©Roy Morsch 1983/The Stock Market: p. 191; ©Felicia Martinez/Photo Edit: p. 193; ©Ron Routar 1991/FPG International: p. 230; Peter L. Gould/FPG International: p. 233; ©Michael Simpson 1991/ FPG International: p. 234; Arizona Historical Society Library: p. 247; ©Deborah Davis/Photo Edit: p. 249; ©Margaret Cubberly/Phototake NYC: p. 255; ©Earl Young/FPG International: p. 262; ©CNRI/Phototake NYC: p. 270; Phototake: pp. 281, 655, 835; ©NASA/SB/FPG International: p. 288; The Granger Collection, New York: p. 292; ©1991 Brownie Harris/The Stock Market: p. 296; UPI/Bettmann Newsphotos: pp. 300, 847; ©1985 Paul Ambrose/FPG International: p. 304; ©Tom Carroll 1988/FPG International: p. 306; ©Spencer Grant/FPG International: pp. 309, 586; FPG International: p. 323; ©Frank Rossotto/The Stock Market: pp. 328, 925; Archive Photos/Orville Logan Snider: p. 337; Magnum Photos: p. 338; ©Dennis Kunkel/CNRI/Phototake NYC: p. 347; ©Art Montes De Oca 1989/ FPG International: p. 348; Mary Evans Picture Library: pp. 351, 1025; ©Dr. Louise Chow/Phototake NYC: p. 353; Cold Spring Harbor Laboratory Archives: p. 354; Reuters/Bettmann Newsphotos: p. 367; ©Dr. David Rosenbaum/Phototake NYC: p. 383; Bill Wisser/FPG International: p. 386; National Portrait Gallery, London: p. 387; ©Jeff Greenberg/Photo Edit: p. 395; ©Tom Campbell 1989/FPG International: p. 397; Bob Abraham/The Stock Market: pp. 408, 641; ©Spencer Jones 1993/FPG International: p. 463; Michael Price/FPG International: p. 473; ©Gabe Palmer/Kane, Inc. 1982/The Stock Market: p. 475; Anthony Howarth/Science Photo Library/Photo Researchers, Inc.: p. 482; Thomas Lindsay/FPG International: p. 509; Illustration from *Levitating Trains and Kamikaze Genes: Technological Literacy for the 1990's,* by Richard P. Brennan. Copyright © 1990 by John Wiley & Sons, Inc. Reprinted by permission of John Wiley & Sons, Inc.: p. 513; ©Holt Confer/Phototake NYC: p. 514; ©Miriam Berkley: p. 526; Michael Johnson; courtesy of Green-Peace: p. 534; ©1990 Jack Van Antwerp/The Stock Market: p. 536; E. Bernstein and E. Kairinen, Gillette Research Institute: p. 540; ©Carolina Biological Supp/Phototake NYC: p. 545; National Museum of

Medicine: p. 576; ©1987 Randy Duchaine/The Stock Market: p. 592; ©1993 John Olson/The Stock Market: p. 597; ©1988 Don Mason/The Stock Market: p. 642; ©1991 Ken Korsh/FPG International: p. 643; ©Granada Studios/FPG International: p. 644; ©Ron Routar 1991/FPG International: p. 646; Arthur Gurman Kin/Phototake NYC: p. 652; Tom McCarthy Photos/Photo Edit: p. 659; ©Robert Reiff 1991/FPG International: p. 667; ©R. Rathe 1993/FPG International: p. 671; ©J. Barry O'Rourke/The Stock Market: p. 673; ©Kent Knudson 1991/FPG International: p. 675; ©1994 Eugene Smith/Black Star: p. 686; NASA: pp. 687, 728, 769, 903, 986, 991, 992, 999; Dick Kent Photography/FPG International: p. 691; ©Frank Rossotto 1992/The Stock Market: p. 693; ©Jack Zehrt 1992/FPG International: p. 711; ©Leslye Borden/Photo Edit: p. 719; ©Peter Vadnai/The Stock Market: p. 736; ©Overseas/Phototake NYC: p. 750; ©Paul Ambrose 1988/ FPG International: p. 751; Robert Visser; courtesy of GreenPeace: p. 754; ©Steve McCutcheon/Visuals Unlimited: p. 758; ©Peter Britton/Phototake NYC: p. 759; ©Zachary Singer/GreenPeace 1989: p. 761; NASA/Phototake: pp. 772, 1004; ©Mauritus GMBH/Phototake NYC: p. 808; ©Michael Seigel/Phototake NYC: p. 818; LeKarer; courtesy of GreenPeace: p. 822; USGS: p. 844; John Gajda/FPG International: p. 857; ©1991 Howard Sochurek/The Stock Market: p. 859; ©1991 Peter Beck/The Stock Market: p. 884; ©Robert Ginn/Photo Edit: p. 894; ©Peter Gridley 1987/FPG International: p. 896; ©John Madere/The Stock Market: p. 898; ©Steve Kahn 1990/FPG International: p. 899; ©Paul Ambrose 1986/FPG International: p. 924; Tass/Sovfoto: p. 988; ©Jeff Divine 1991/FPG International: p. 1037; ©1994 Peggy and Ronald Barnett/The Stock Market: p. 1050; ©Movie Still Archives 1994/FPG International: p. 1065; ©Gabe Palmer/The Stock Market: p. 1068; ©Phototake Kunkel/Phototake NYC: p. 1069; Courtesy of I.G.D. Dunlap: p. 1072; Indianapolis & Louisville Ry.: p. 1081; UP: p. 1084; ©AAA Photo/Phototake NYC: p. 1085; ©Ann Chwatsky/Phototake NYC: p. 1091; Courtesy of The Mark Twain Papers, Bancroft Library: p. 1103; ©Richard Nowitz 1990/ FPG International: p. 1109; ©Wagner Herbert Stock/Phototake NYC: p. 1133; ©1988 Jim Brown/The Stock Market: p. 1146; ©Peter A. Simon/Phototake NYC: pp. 926, 1155; Royal Institution: p. 1161.

The original illustrations appearing in *Eureka!* were researched and drawn by Teresa SanClementi.

Eureka!

⋆⋆ Cable television

Cable television was first known as CATV (community antenna television) and was used to deliver a clear signal to rural communities. At the time, a CATV system generally consisted of a single large antenna mounted in a high, clear area to receive signals from distant TV broadcasters. Cables were fed to the houses in the community and usually delivered two or three channels.

The Commercial Potential of Cable TV

In the mid-1960s, new technology allowed for up to 12 channels to be carried through a single cable. In order to fill these new channels, cable operators began to bring in television signals from more distant sources. This allowed viewers to watch stations from large cities and neighboring states. With access to a wider variety of stations, the demand for cable increased.

Apart from dramatically improved reception, cable television could offer educational, cultural, and community service programs, since cable systems could be bidirectional, or interactive. That is, from their homes viewers could use their cable television to answer questions or participate in polls, among other things.

In the early 1970s, several small companies in California and on the East Coast began offering pay-per-view broadcasting: first-run films and major sporting events delivered by cable to a viewer's home for a monthly fee. The popularity of these programs caused demand to skyrocket, and by 1975 the first nationwide pay-per-view cable station—Home Box Office (HBO)—was in service.

Apart from dramatically improved reception, cable television could offer educational, cultural, and community service programs.

An illustration of Europe's first direct broadcast television satellite. Communication satellites often feed the microwave dishes that deliver signals to cable systems.

How Cable TV Works

What makes cable transmission practical is its use of coaxial cable. This thick, layered cable allows transmission of a wide band of frequencies and rejects interference from automobiles and electrical appliances.

As coaxial technology improved, the number of stations available to cable operators rose from 12 to more than 50, and now that number can be increased to almost 150. The antennas once used to deliver a signal to a cable system are long since gone, replaced by microwave dishes often fed by **communications satellites**.

Once a signal is delivered to a cable company in this manner, it is distributed over cable lines to customers. Broadcasts are often scrambled to prevent non-subscribers from splicing into a cable line without paying for the service.

Viewers today prefer cable's clear image, which is unaffected by poor weather conditions and most types of interference. Optimists still await true bidirectionality (interactive TV) that would allow viewers to do their banking, grocery shopping, and perhaps even their voting via their cable systems.

As a multichannel carrier, cable seems to be the ideal medium for the introduction of high-definition television (also called HDTV or Hi-Def), because HDTV must use two channels' worth of information layered on top of each other to produce its theater-quality picture. And, should **fiber optic** cable replace coaxial, a nearly infinite number of stations could be carried.

See also **Fiber optics**

⋆⋆ Calculable function

Algorithms have become one of the basic concepts in mathematics as well as an important component of **cybernetics** and **digital computer** programming. (Cybernetics is the study of how people and machines interact.) Algorithms denote an exact procedure or set of rules used to solve a problem or complete a task. Some of our most familiar algorithms are the rules for elementary mathematics—addition, subtraction, multiplication, and division.

In the 1930s, many mathematicians began to explore the solvability and unsolvability of algorithmic problems. Particularly important is the work done in this area by Alonso Church. Born in 1903, Church was educated at Princeton University, where he later joined the staff as chairman of mathematics and philosophy. He remained at Princeton for 40 years and also held a similar position at the University of California.

In 1936 Church was the first to establish proof that there were no algorithms for a class of quite elementary arithmetical questions. This provided the first precise definition of a calculable function, and the discovery contributed enormously to the development of computing algorithms.

The English mathematician Alan Turing (1912-1954) performed similar work to that of Church. Their combined theories are known as the Church-Turing thesis.

A replica of the mechanical calculator built by French scientist and philosopher Blaise Pascal in 1652. Three hundred years later the microchip would revolutionize calculating machines.

⋆⋆ Calculator, pocket

Within a few years of its invention in 1959, the integrated circuit (microchip)—tiny, complex electronic circuits on a single chip of silicon—had become reliable and inexpensive. The president of Texas Instruments (TI), Patrick Haggerty, wanted to demonstrate the unlimited uses of the inte-

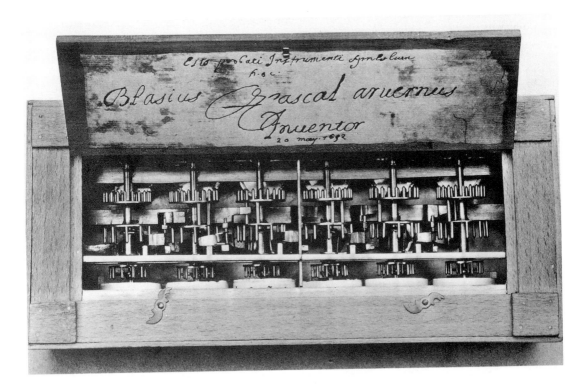

William Seward Burroughs, American Inventor

The forerunner of the pocket calculator was created in the late 1890s in the United States by William Seward Burroughs (1855-1898).

Born in Auburn, New York, Burroughs began tinkering in his father's machine shop early in his childhood. It was a hobby he continued throughout most of his life. While he was working in a bank at age 15, Burroughs imagined a machine that would perform arithmetical calculation. Such a machine, the Comptometer developed by Eugene Felt (1862-1930), was successfully used by most businesses of that time. But Burroughs wanted to design a calculator that could print figures as they were entered, thus permitting greater permanency and accuracy.

In 1881 Burroughs moved to St. Louis, Missouri, and began developing the device in his spare time. Three years later he had a working model and his first patent. Once in production, however, his machine design proved impractical. With help from his three partners, Burroughs sold $100,000 of stock in the American Arithmetic Company and continued with his experimentation. His second design was also unsuccessful because it was unable to stand up to heavy use.

Finally in 1891, Burroughs produced a well-designed, fully functional adding machine. Each figure entered and the final results of the computation were printed on paper. Burroughs enlisted the Boyer Machine Company to help in production.

The adding machine proved a great success, particularly in banking and insurance offices. Burroughs died in 1898 before he could see the impact his machine had on improving the efficiency and accuracy of the business world. In 1905 the American Arithmetic Company was renamed the Burroughs Adding Machine Company (later shortened to Burroughs Corporation) and moved operations to Detroit, Michigan. Burroughs, now a part of Unisys, continues to be a worldwide leader in the field.

grated circuit, which was then mostly used for military and industrial functions. In October 1965 Haggerty challenged Jack Kilby, a TI engineer and co-inventor of the microchip, to design a miniature calculator that would be as powerful as desk models but small enough to fit into a coat pocket.

Kilby Responds to the Challenge

Kilby was a man who thrived on solving difficult technical problems. He assembled a three-man team of himself and two other TI engineers that produced a prototype (early model) within a year. Jerry Merryman, a self-taught electrical engineer, designed the logic circuits to fit within the power and space limitations. James Van Tassel, an expert on semiconductor components (parts), developed a small, power-efficient keyboard for the input. Kilby found a suitable rechargeable battery.

Displaying the output remained a problem. **LED (light-emitting diode)** technology, which has become the standard for calculator display, was not yet advanced enough to use. So Kilby invented a new thermal printer with a low-power printing head that pressed the paper readout against a heated digit.

A common solar-powered calculator with LED readout. The electronic pocket calculator surprised its inventors by appealing not just to business people, engineers, and scientists, but also to average consumers.

Kilby, Merryman, and Van Tassel applied for a patent on their "Miniature Electronic Calculator" in 1967. Because the pocket calculator was an entirely new device, it took some years to get it into production.

TI formed a joint venture with the Canon company of Tokyo and placed the Pocketronic Printing Calculator on the market in the United States in 1971. It was not nearly as portable and cheap as today's models: the Pocketronic weighed two pounds and cost $150.

But it was an immediate success. Like the other electronic pocket calculators that soon began appearing, it surprised its inventors by appealing not just to business people, engineers, and scientists, but also to average consumers. They used the devices to total grocery bills, figure square footage of rooms, prepare income tax forms, and do other common mathematical tasks.

Hewlett-Packard Enters the Market

Improved models soon followed. In 1972 Hewlett-Packard introduced the HP-35. It was the first handheld scientific calculator, and it featured LED display. Also in 1972, TI marketed the Datamath, which used a single chip and had a full-floating decimal point, LED display, and limited memory.

Today, pocket calculators with a wide range of functions are available, including programmable calculators that are in effect miniature computers. More than 50 million portable calculators are now sold in the United States each year, many for less than $10.

In 1975 the Smithsonian Institution in Washington, D.C., made the original pocket calculator part of its permanent collection. In 1976 Keuffel & Esser, manufacturer of millions of slide rules over the years, presented its last slide rule to the Smithsonian. The pocket calculator had made slide rule technology obsolete.

⋆⋆⋆ Canal and canal lock

Canals—artificial waterways—are deep ditches that are dug to redirect water from lakes and rivers to help with transportation, to irrigate or drain land, and to supply water. Irrigation canals were found in most ancient civilizations. The Nahrwan Canal, 185 miles (300 km) long, was built between the Tigris and Euphrates Rivers about 2400 B.C., and Egypt's pharaohs linked the Mediterranean and Red Seas with a canal that the Romans later restored and used for shipping. China built the first stretch of its Grand Canal in A.D. 610, a waterway 600 miles (1,000 km) long when completed.

Transportation

Canal systems for transportation were not widespread in Europe until the 1600s and 1700s. Cargo boats used in the canal systems were designed with flat bottoms to accommodate the shallow depths.

Changes in land levels are a primary concern in canal construction because canal bottoms must be flat. Lake Erie, for example, is roughly 325 feet (99.125 m) higher than Lake Ontario. The modern method for compensating for different levels is the lock—a chamber linking different water levels. Boats enter and leave the lock through a pair of gates. When both gates are closed, the water level in the chamber is raised or lowered, taking the boats to the desired level.

Today many of Western Europe's major rivers are linked by a huge canal system used for shipping. In the United States, the opening of the

Boats enter and leave a lock through a pair of gates. When both gates are closed, the water level in the chamber is raised or lowered (as illustrated here), taking the boats to the desired level.

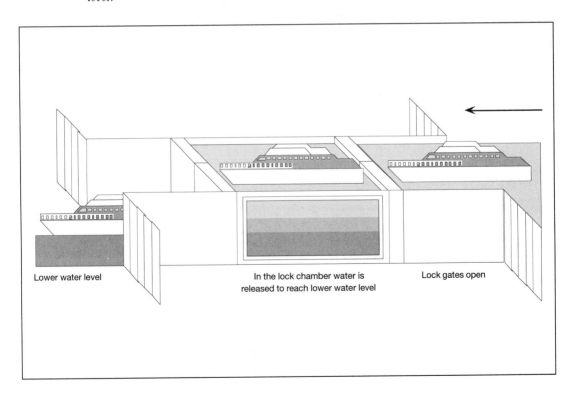

Lower water level

In the lock chamber water is released to reach lower water level

Lock gates open

Erie Canal in 1825 signaled the onset of a national water transportation network. Its success spurred construction of canals in such cities as Philadelphia and Washington, D.C., although by the 1860s railroads were replacing canals for shipping and transportation.

Engineering Feats

Canal construction reached its technological peak when canals began accommodating oceangoing vessels. These ships require depths of 30 to 40 feet (9.15 to 12.2 m). To justify the cost and effort involved, deep-water canals either must offer an alternative to lengthy shipping routes, as do the Suez Canal in Egypt (1869) and the Panama Canal in Central America (1914), or permit access to inland ports. The Suez Canal allows ships to travel from Europe to Asia without circling the African continent. The Panama Canal permits access from the Atlantic to the Pacific Ocean without circling the South American continent. Completion of the St. Lawrence Seaway allowed ocean access to the inland Great Lakes ports.

The Gatun Locks of the Panama Canal. To justify their expense, deep-water canals must offer an alternative to lengthy shipping routes (as does the Panama Canal) or permit access to inland ports.

⋆ Can and canned food

Like freezing, drying, and salting, canning is a method of **food preservation**. In canning, food is heated in a container to the point where all microorganisms that cause spoilage are destroyed. Then the container is completely sealed so no new microorganisms can invade the food. With canning, foods can be kept indefinitely and taken anywhere.

The French Invent Canning

The invention of canning is credited to Nicolas François Appert, a French chef and confectioner (candy maker). He filled loosely corked glass bottles and jars with food, immersed the bottled food in boiling water for certain amounts of time, and then tightly sealed the containers. Appert started a bottling plant in 1804 and won a 12,000-franc prize from the French government for his method in 1809. When Appert published a detailed description of his process in 1810, the canning industry became possible.

Englishman Peter Durand patented an improved version of Appert's process in 1810 using tin-plate canisters instead of glass. (Appert had probably used glass because the tin-plate industry in France at that time was primitive; in England it was flourishing.) In Britain the term "tin canister" was shortened to "tin," in the United States, to "can." That's why British consumers buy "tinned meat," while their American counterparts purchase "canned meat."

Foods can be canned in metal, glass, or plastic containers. With canning, foods can be kept indefinitely and taken anywhere.

Durand's patent was bought in 1811 by Bryan Donkin and John Hall, who established Britain's first cannery in 1812 and began supplying canned goods to the Royal Navy and various Arctic expeditions. By 1830 canned goods were offered for sale to the public in British shops. Canned meat was shipped to England from Australia beginning in 1847.

The British canning industry suffered a series of setbacks starting in 1845, when Stephen Goldner canned soups for John Franklin's Arctic expedition in extra-large containers. Much of the soup went bad. In 1850 over 110,000 pounds of Goldner's tinned meat was condemned. And in 1855 a large shipment of canned food for British troops in the Crimea was found to be spoiled. Public suspicion of canned goods resulted from these well-publicized problems and persisted through the rest of the century.

Canning in the United States

Canning was started in the United States about 1819 by William Underwood in Boston, Massachusetts, and by Thomas Kensett and Ezra Daggett in New York. Underwood packed fruits, pickles, and condiments in bottles. Kensett and Daggett packed salmon, lobsters, and oysters in tin-plate containers that were patented in 1825.

Women working at a fruit cannery in 1930s England. The British canning industry suffered a series of setbacks starting in 1845, when Stephen Goldner canned soups for John Franklin's Arctic expedition in extra-large containers. Much of the soup went bad.

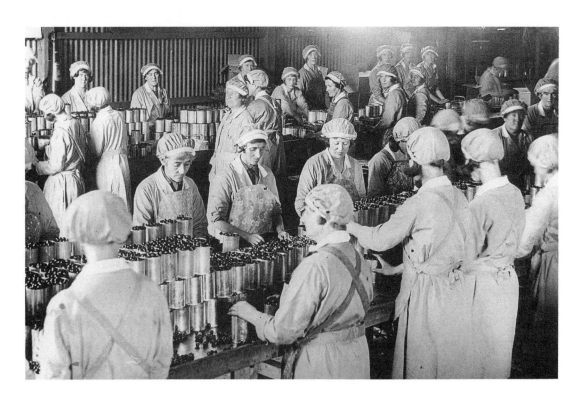

*Borden's milk
and other
canned
products were
used extensively
by Union forces
during the Civil
War.*

Sterilization Makes Canning Possible

Even though all of these advances in canning methods were made in the second half of the nineteenth century, the scientific basis for sterilization remained a mystery until the work of Louis Pasteur (1822-1895) became widely known and accepted. Pasteur's investigations in the 1850s, however, were preceded by the experiments of the Italian scientist Lazzaro Spallanzani (1729-1799) a century earlier. Spallanzani had boiled foods, such as gravy, for extended amounts of time and sealed them. No new microorganisms grew.

In his 1860s study of fermentation, Pasteur disclosed the role of microorganisms in food spoilage and the use of heat to kill these organisms, thus preventing spoilage. This explained the massive spoilage of British canned goods around 1850. The heat had been unable to penetrate all the way to the center of the extra-large cans, so food in the center remained unsterilized.

Using Pasteur's discoveries, it was now possible to develop scientific standards for food sterilization. In 1895 Henry Russell of the University of Wisconsin showed that gas-producing **bacteria** can cause spoilage of canned goods. However, longer processing times at higher temperatures killed these bacteria. Samuel Prescott and William Underwood (grandson of the pioneer canner) of the Massachusetts Institute of Technology identified many such bacteria and specified time and temperature requirements for high- and low-acid foods. They began to publish their findings in 1897.

Seafood canning was established in Maine in 1843, and Lafayette College students enjoyed canned tomatoes in 1847. Gail Borden canned a sweetened condensed milk in 1856. Borden's milk and other canned products were used extensively by Union (Northern) forces during the Civil War (1861-65). Salmon was canned in California in 1864, meats in Chicago in 1872, and sardines in Maine in 1876.

Technological Offshoots

The increased demand for foodstuffs created by the expanding canning industry gave rise to other inventions between 1893 and 1903, such as the picking-and-shelling machine for peas, the automatic corn cutter, and a device that gutted, deheaded, de-tailed, and chopped salmon.

The major technical developments in canning in the nineteenth century occurred in processing methods and can manufacture. Nicolas François Appert had used an autoclave, a primitive sort of pressure cooker. In 1854 Raymond Chevallier Appert added pressure gauges to autoclaves for better control. An alternative processing method was the calcium chloride bath, patented in Britain in 1841 by Stephen Goldner and J. Wertheimer.

Both the autoclave and calcium chloride bath allowed foods to be processed at temperatures higher than boiling water, thus reducing processing time. The steam retort (pressure cooker) introduced in 1874 further reduced sterilization time.

The can with locked side seams and double end seams (a type used today) was machine made as early as 1824 in England. Following the granting of U.S. patents for a rubber composition that made perfect end joints, modern "sanitary" or open-topped cans without soldering appeared around 1905.

Home canning has always involved glass containers. John L. Mason, an American glass blower, patented in 1858 his glass canning jar with a threaded top for the screw-on caps. Mason jars are still widely used for home canning.

Modern Methods

The modern tin can is 98.5 percent sheet-steel thinly coated with tin. Cans for certain foods that react with tin are coated inside with enamel. Since World War II, lightweight aluminum cans have been used for some food products. Both flexible and rigid **plastic** containers are now being developed for canning.

While most foods today are canned using the traditional sterilization of pressure cooking, some processes use the direct-flame sterilization of rotating cans, or the aseptic canning process in which cans are filled with pre-sterilized food in a germ-free environment.

See also **Germ theory**

⋆⋆ Can opener

Curiously, the first patent for a can opener was issued 48 years after Peter Durand secured his 1810 patent for the tin can. It was not as though the can opener was an unneeded invention! A tin of roast veal taken on William Parry's voyage to the Arctic in 1824 instructed: "Cut round on the top near to the outer edge with a chisel and hammer."

The hammer-and-chisel or screwdriver method of getting to a can's contents was finally made obsolete in 1858 when Ezra J. Warner of Waterbury, Connecticut, patented his can opener. The device used a long blade or spike to pierce the can and a shorter blade to grasp the container's rim. During the Civil War (1861-65), Union (Northern) troops received Warner's can opener along with their rations of canned food.

Many can openers were patented from the 1860s through the turn of the century, some designed for multiple uses. A notable 1878 patent design by J. Cox was a "combined can opener, knife and scissor sharpener, tack drawer, putty knife, tack hammer; complete with finger rests."

The modern type of can opener, with a cutting wheel instead of a spike or blade turned by a crank, was introduced in 1878. However, can openers did not become popular until wall-mounted models appeared in 1930. The electric can opener was introduced in 1957.

See also **Can and canned food**

⁎⋆ Carbon

The soot produced by the burning camp fires of the earliest cave people consisted of nearly pure carbon.

No element occurs in such diverse forms or in so many different compounds as does carbon. Humans have encountered and used carbon and its compounds since the early days of history. The soot produced by the burning camp fires of the earliest cave people consisted of nearly pure carbon. References to coal, asphalt, bitumen, **petroleum**, and **natural gas**—all forms of carbon or compounds of carbon—go back at least to Biblical times.

For example, a Greek historian tells in 400 B.C. of a natural gas well in ancient Turkey that provided a "perpetual flame" for religious ceremonies. Also, around 320 B.C. Theophrastus of Eresus discussed a mineral that was probably lignite, a type of coal. We also know that people of Biblical times mixed lampblack, a form of carbon, with olive oil and balsam gum to make a primitive form of ink. Diamonds, another form of pure carbon, are described in the literature of most early societies, including the Bible (Middle East) and ancient Hindu (East Indian) scriptures.

The Science of Carbon

A great deal of confusion surrounded the various forms of carbon. Scholars found it difficult to believe that lampblack, coal, graphite, and diamond could all be different forms of the same element. Even when some forms of carbon—charcoal and coke, for example—were acknowledged to be elementary, doubt remained about the status of diamond. It seemed difficult to accept the fact that charcoal and diamond differed only in the arrangement of atoms.

Carbon forms more compounds than all other elements combined. The number of such compounds runs into the millions and increases by at least a few hundred thousand every year. The explanation for this phenomenon is the chemical ability of carbon atoms to bond with each other in seemingly endless chains which, in turn, may assume a staggeringly large variety of conformations. For example, the relatively simple hydrocarbon known as decane can theoretically exist in 75 different forms or **isomers**.

All organic compounds, by definition, contain carbon. In addition, some major inorganic compounds—**carbon dioxide**, **carbon monoxide**, and the carbonates—include the element.

A carbon atom. Carbon atoms form more compounds than all other elements combined because of their chemical ability to bond with each other in seemingly endless chains.

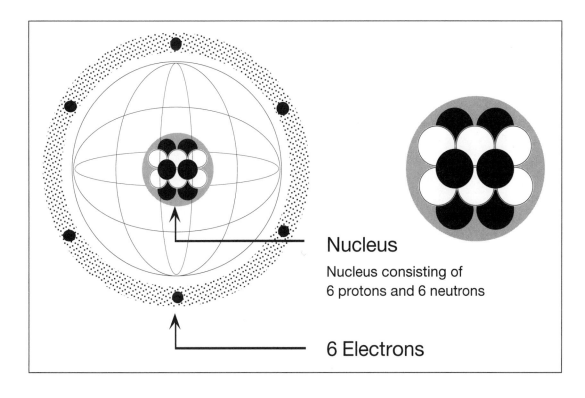

Nucleus

Nucleus consisting of 6 protons and 6 neutrons

6 Electrons

Carbon makes up about 0.027 percent of the Earth's crust. The element has also been found in the **Sun**, in other stars, in comets, and in the atmosphere of most planets. Some meteorites contain carbon in the form of microscopic diamonds.

Because of their natural beauty and hardness, diamonds have always been highly prized. They occur naturally in the remnants of ancient volcanic flows, buried miles below Earth's surface. They have also been found in certain locations on the ocean floor. Scientists had long tried to find ways to manufacture synthetic diamonds from other forms of carbon and finally made one from graphite placed under enormous pressure in 1954.

While most gem diamonds are still natural products, the majority of diamonds used in industry are made synthetically.

Commercial Uses of Carbon Forms

The properties of elemental carbon vary dramatically. Graphite, for example, is one of the softest materials known, while diamond is the hardest naturally occurring substance.

Graphite is used in the manufacture of "lead" pencils, pigments, lubricants, electrodes for carbon-arc lamps and electrochemical cells, refractory crucibles, matches and explosives, and moderators used in nuclear reactors.

Commercial diamonds are used in the manufacture of devices for drilling, polishing, grinding, and cutting other materials. Dies used to shape or finish materials in the manufacture of **tungsten** and other hard wires as well as parts for delicate instruments are often made of diamond.

Other carbon forms are used for deodorizing and decolorizing materials, in inks, dyes, and pigments, in electrical equipment, and in some medicines.

⋆⋆ Carbon dioxide

Carbon dioxide (CO_2) was the first gas to be distinguished from ordinary air, perhaps because it is so closely connected with the cycles of plant and animal life. When we breathe air or when we burn wood and other fuels, carbon dioxide is released. When plants store energy in the form of food, they use up carbon dioxide. Early scientists were able to observe the effects of carbon dioxide long before they knew exactly what it was.

Around 1630 Flemish scientist Jan van Helmont discovered that certain vapors differed from air, which was then thought to be a single substance or **element**. Van Helmont coined the term "gas" to describe these vapors and collected the gas given off by burning wood, calling it "gas sylvestre." Today we know this gas to be carbon dioxide, and van Helmont is credited with its discovery.

Van Helmont also recognized that carbon dioxide was produced by the **fermentation** of wine and from other natural processes. Before long, other scientists began to notice similarities between the processes of breathing (respiration) and burning (**combustion**). Both use up **oxygen** and both give off carbon dioxide. For example, a candle flame will eventually be extinguished when enclosed in a jar with a limited supply of air. The flame dies without oxygen as will a bird or small animal enclosed in an airless jar.

Then in 1756, Joseph Black demonstrated that carbon dioxide, which he called "fixed air," is present in the atmosphere and that it combines with other chemicals to form compounds. Black also identified carbon dioxide in exhaled breath and determined that the gas is heavier than air. He characterized its chemical behavior as that of a weak **acid**. The pioneering work of van Helmont and Black soon led to the discovery of other gases. Chemists soon realized that gases must be weighed and accounted for in the analysis of chemical compounds, just like solids and liquids.

Soda Pop Is Discovered

The first practical use for carbon dioxide was artificially carbonated water (also called soda water or seltzer). Carbon dioxide is still used today to make colas and other soft drinks. In addition to supplying bubbles and zest, the gas acts as a preservative.

Around the late 1780s, chemists began making the connection between carbon dioxide and plant life. Like animals, plants "breathe,"

Recently, carbon dioxide has received negative attention as a "greenhouse" gas. When it accumulates in the upper atmosphere, it traps the Earth's heat, which could eventually cause global warming.

using up oxygen and releasing carbon dioxide. But plants also have the unique ability to store energy in the form of carbohydrates, our primary source of food. This energy-storing process, called **photosynthesis**, is essentially the reverse of respiration. It uses up carbon dioxide and releases oxygen in a complex series of reactions that also require sunlight and chlorophyll (the green substance that gives plants their color).

Since these early discoveries, chemists have learned much more about carbon dioxide. The decay of all organic materials produces carbon dioxide very slowly, and Earth's atmosphere contains a small amount of the gas (about 0.033 percent). In our solar system, the planets of **Venus** and **Mars** have atmospheres very rich in carbon dioxide. The gas also exists in ocean water, where it plays a vital role in marine plant photosynthesis.

Since the beginning of the Industrial Revolution in the mid-1700s, factories and power plants have significantly increased the amount of carbon dioxide in the atmosphere by burning coal and other fossil fuels.

Industrial Uses

In modern life, carbon dioxide has many practical applications. For example, fire extinguishers use CO_2 to control electrical and oil fires, which cannot be put out with water. Because carbon dioxide is heavier than air, it spreads into a blanket and smothers the flames.

Carbon dioxide is also a very effective refrigerant. In its solid form, known as "dry ice," it is used to chill perishable food during transport. Many industrial processes are also cooled by carbon dioxide, which allows faster production rates.

CO₂ Tied to Greenhouse Effect

Recently, carbon dioxide has received negative attention as a "greenhouse" gas. When it accumulates in the upper atmosphere, it traps the Earth's heat, which could eventually cause global warming. Since the beginning of the Industrial Revolution in the mid-1700s, factories and power plants have significantly increased the amount of carbon dioxide in the atmosphere by burning coal and other fossil fuels.

The Greenhouse Effect was first predicted by Svante August Arrhenius, a Swedish physicist, in the 1880s. Modern scientists have confirmed this view and identified other causes of increasing carbon dioxide levels, such as the clearing of the world's forests. Trees extract CO_2 from the air and their disappearance has contributed to upsetting the delicate balance of gases in the atmosphere.

In very rare circumstances, carbon dioxide can endanger life. In 1986 a huge cloud of carbon dioxide exploded from Lake Nyos, a volcanic lake in northwestern Cameroon (Africa), and quickly suffocated more than 1,700 people and 8,000 animals. Today, scientists are attempting to control this phenomenon by slowly pumping the gas up from the bottom of the lake.

✦ Carbon monoxide

Most people are aware that carbon monoxide is a very dangerous gas. If a car is left running in an unventilated area, carbon monoxide from the exhaust fumes can rapidly climb to deadly levels. Carbon monoxide gas can also accumulate in a house if the furnace is defective or if the chimney is clogged. Because carbon monoxide causes drowsiness and has no odor, taste, or color, people often fall asleep without knowing that they are being poisoned.

Poison

In the 1300s, Arnold of Villanova (1235-1311), a Spanish scientist, noticed that poisonous fumes were produced when wood burned without

Because carbon monoxide causes drowsiness and has no odor, taste, or color, people often fall asleep without knowing that they are being poisoned.

In large cities, unhealthy amounts of carbon monoxide can build up, especially during heavy rush-hour traffic. Cars that are old give off the most carbon monoxide.

adequate ventilation. During the 1600s and 1700s, scientists began to learn more about the nature of gases. During this period of discovery, French chemist Joseph Marie François de Lassone (1717-1788) and British chemist Joseph Priestley (1733-1804) independently prepared carbon monoxide gas in the laboratory for the first time. Soon afterward, in 1800, British chemist William Cumberland Cruikshank (1745-1800) determined its chemical composition.

However, carbon monoxide's poisonous effects were not well understood until the 1850s, when Claude Bernard, a French physiologist, explained how the gas acts in the human body. Bernard showed that when we breathe carbon monoxide, the gas prevents our **blood** from carrying oxygen through the body.

Pollution

Normally, carbon monoxide is present in the air in tiny amounts which are not large enough to pose a threat. However, in large cities, unhealthy amounts of carbon monoxide can build up, especially during heavy rush-hour traffic. Cars that are old give off the most carbon monoxide. Modern cars are equipped with catalytic converters that chemically change carbon monoxide into carbon dioxide.

Despite its dangers, carbon monoxide is useful to industry as a fuel gas that provides heat for manufacturing processes and serves as a raw material for making chemicals and purifying such metals as **iron** and nickel.

⋆⋆⋆ Carcinogen

Cancer is a mysterious group of over 100 different types of diseases. These can be distinguished by the type of cell or organ which is affected, the treatment plan employed, and the cause of the cancer. Anything that can cause cancer is called a carcinogen.

Anything that can cause cancer is called a carcinogen.

Today, the media rarely miss an opportunity to report on newly discovered carcinogenic substances. Sometimes it seems as if *everything* causes cancer, but very few things are proven carcinogens. The two main categories of carcinogens include genetic and environmental factors.

Environmental Carcinogens

Specific environmental factors include tobacco, alcohol, diet, infection, sexual practices, occupation, geophysical phenomena, pollution, med-

Tobacco Is a Carcinogen

The U.S. Surgeon General estimates that 30 percent of all cancer deaths are directly attributable to the use of tobacco. The carcinogens in tobacco include nicotine and tar.

Pipe and cigar smoke contain essentially the same array of poisons although the amounts may vary. Second-hand tobacco smoke, whatever the source, should also be considered as a major carcinogen.

Smokeless tobacco, including chewing tobacco and snuff, are not alternatives to avoid cancer because these products contain large quantities of other cancer-causing chemicals. Lip, mouth, tongue, and throat cancers have been positively linked to the use of smokeless tobacco products.

The risk of these types of cancers are increased when tobacco is used with alcohol. This phenomenon is known as "synergism." While marijuana does not contain nicotine or tobacco, it does contain tar and other carcinogens.

ications, food additives, and industrial products. Tobacco and diet together account for almost two-thirds of all cancer-related deaths. Stress and emotional factors should be listed as elements that may contribute toward the development of some cancers. Cigarette smoking is clearly the single most preventable cause of illness and premature death in the United States.

Diet and nutrition have been recognized as major factors that influence the development of many cancers. The National Cancer Institute recommends a low-fat, high-fiber diet. Vegetables such as cabbage and brussels sprouts may help reduce the chances of developing some stomach and colon cancers. Charred foods and alcohol should be avoided or consumed in moderation.

Infection may also lead to cancer. This usually occurs when a **virus**, **bacteria**, or parasite is contracted. Only about 10 percent of all cancers are believed to be caused by these organisms. Retroviruses such as the herpes virus and the virus that causes **AIDS** have been tied to certain types of cancer. Retroviruses can enter directly into a host's genetic material and reproduce themselves.

Radiation from the **Sun** is another environmental carcinogen. It is an increasing concern due to the depletion of the protective **ozone** layer in the

Earth's upper atmosphere. The Sun is now the chief cause of non-melanoma skin cancer, or cancers that do not take the form of darkly pigmented tumors. The amount of ultraviolet-beta radiation from the Sun varies with location, altitude, sky cover, and the time of year. Exposure levels can be reduced by using sunscreen products and monitoring prolonged outdoor activities—especially between 11:00 A.M. and 1:00 P.M. during the late summer months.

Changes in the body resulting from sexual intercourse, pregnancy, and childbirth are obviously in a different class of carcinogens than those produced by exposure to chemicals. They are, however, considered environmental since they are not controlled only by one's own genes.

This is not to suggest that childbirth causes cancer. In fact, pregnancy and childbirth may actually help prevent cancer of the uterus, ovary, and breast. However, frequent sexual intercourse with large numbers of partners has been positively linked to an increased risk of cervical cancer. Researchers think that the primary carcinogenic agent in this example may actually be an unknown virus.

Some jobs have cancer-related dangers. Coal miners may develop "black lung" from breathing coal dust.

Work-Related Carcinogens

One of the first people to suspect that certain substances in the environment can cause cancer was Sir Percivall Pott (1714-1788), who in 1775 published a paper on cancer rates in chimney sweeps. It has since been discovered that benzo(a)pyrene, a chemical found in soot, is a potent carcinogen.

Other jobs have their own cancer-related dangers. Coal miners may develop "black lung" from breathing coal dust. Asbestos workers develop "white lung" when the asbestos fibers affect their lungs. Workers in paper mills, fertilizer plants, and dry cleaners may also be exposed to carcinogens in dust or fumes.

Genetic Predisposition

Most environmental carcinogens are avoidable. Genetically predisposed cancers are more difficult to control. They are also less common than many environmentally induced cancers. Early diagnosis and treatment increases the recovery rate for all cancers.

₊ Cargo ship

The first freighter hauled iron ore on the Great Lakes during the late 1800s. It resembled a long steel box, with crew quarters at the front and engine at the back.

Cargo ships bring food, medicine, and products to every port on the planet. There are two basic kinds of cargo ships: freighters and tankers.

Freighters

Freighters come in all shapes and sizes. Dry cargo vessels transport loose goods such as coal, grain, iron ore, and similar products that can be loaded in bulk. Modern freighters have a double hull for strength and safety, and include storage areas for fuel oil, water ballast (weight), or fresh water. The largest of these freighters in use today, with the bridge and engine room near the tail, can haul more than 100,000 tons of cargo. Barges are smaller forms of these bulk carriers. Formerly powered by sail, they now have diesel engines or are towed by tugboats.

General cargo vessels haul packaged items. During World War II (1939-45), the United States built many cargo vessels, called Liberty and

Victory ships, which transported troops and supplies throughout the world. Modern cargo ships house powerful, electrically driven cranes and derricks. These ships can be loaded from the side and stern as well as from the hatches. They also have automatic engine and navigational controls.

Tankers

The second kind of cargo ship is the tanker. In 1878 Ludwig Nobel revolutionized the way oil was carried. Previous to his time, all liquids were transported in barrels or tanks, but Nobel's idea was to launch a ship that itself was one huge tank. The early tankers were 300 feet long with a capacity of 2,300 tons of oil. Today, there are tankers 1,000 feet long that can carry 300,000 tons of oil. Their hulls are divided into tanks, which are loaded or unloaded by pumps.

Because of recent well-known oil spills, such as the Exxon *Valdez* off the coast of Alaska, there are plans for double-hulled construction to prevent such disasters. If one hull is punctured, the second hull still contains the oil. Other tankers can carry liquefied natural gases in specially designed tanks. Space between the gas tanks and the hull is designed to prevent explosions.

A freighter equipped with containers. In 1968 the United States launched its first multipurpose vessel that could carry containers, roll on/roll off cargo, various general cargo, and refrigerated items.

Combined Design

Finally, there are multipurpose ships that combine the features of a freighter and a tanker. Some have refrigerated space for foods that spoil easily. Others have tank space to haul liquids, and a deck for roll on/roll off containers such as barrels. In 1968 the United States launched its first multi-purpose vessel that could carry containers, roll on/roll off cargo, various general cargo, and refrigerated items.

⋆⋆ Carpet

When the word "carpet" is used today, it usually refers to the machine-woven wall-to-wall carpets found in homes and offices. However, the modern carpet has its origins in the hand-woven carpets of England and, before that, the intricate rugs of Persia and the Far East.

Ancient Art Form

The first rugs were probably woven by nomadic (wandering) shepherds. These thick and durable rugs were used as ground coverings, blankets, walls, and doors. Since these nomads had little in the way of music or literature, the patterns displayed on their rugs were their principal art form. As trade between Europe and Asia increased, the rugs of the Far East became very popular. In most cases they were deemed too beautiful to be walked on, and were instead hung on walls or over furniture as decoration.

Until the mid-1800s, all rugs were woven by hand. This was a time-consuming process, since the wool that made up the rug's pattern was knotted through the backing one piece at a time. Generally, rugs with more knots were considered more valuable. Some priceless Oriental rugs contained more than 2,000 knots per square inch. Such rugs were prized in England, where they were considered a status symbol. In Islamic nations they were valued as prayer rugs.

Opposite page: The modern carpet has its origins in the hand-woven carpets of England and, before that, the intricate rugs of Persia and the Far East.

Technology Lends a Hand

In 1839 Scottish inventor James Templeton developed a power loom for the weaving of Asian-style rugs. Just a year later, American inventor Erastus Bigelow perfected the power loom for carpets. Carpets then began to replace rugs as floor covering.

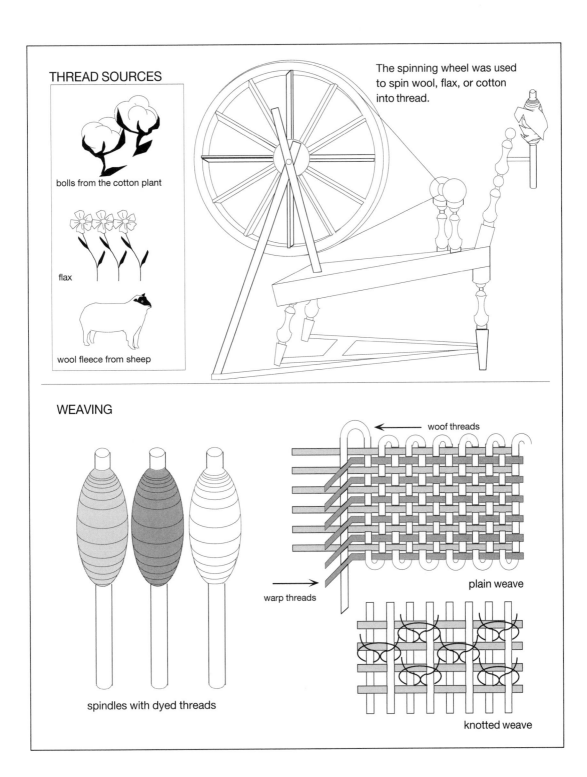

THREAD SOURCES

bolls from the cotton plant

flax

wool fleece from sheep

The spinning wheel was used to spin wool, flax, or cotton into thread.

WEAVING

woof threads

warp threads

plain weave

knotted weave

spindles with dyed threads

Originally, power looms were only 27 inches wide. However, the broad loom was developed in the early 1900s, allowing for the construction of carpets 9 to 18 feet wide. Later looms could produce carpets almost 30 feet wide.

Using a bank of needles, the power carpet looms mimicked the action of hand-weaving. Depending upon the way the yarn was stitched into the warp and weft, different types of carpet could be woven. Popular types included Axminster, Wilton, chenille, and velvet. Rugs and carpets woven on these power looms were popular until just after World War II (1939-45), when they, too, were replaced—this time by tufted carpet.

Most of the carpeting found in homes today is tufted. It is made by stitching yarn through a pre-woven fabric backing. Using hundreds of hollow needles (sometimes more than 1,000), the tufting machine fills the carpet with loops—or tufts—that make up the pile. The carpet's backing is coated with an adhesive, usually latex, to hold the tufts in place. In addition to yarn spun from wool, carpets now are made of synthetic fibers such as **nylon** and **polyester**.

See also **Fiber, synthetic; Mass production**

⋆⋆⋆ Car wash, automatic

The first American car-washing facilities were very expensive to operate because they were labor intensive. They used a conveyor that pulled the car past groups of workers who performed all the tasks associated with cleaning a car.

In the late 1930s, the first fully automatic car wash went into operation in the United States. It had many of the features we recognize today, including large rotating rollers with flexible strands to flick away the dirt. One horizontal roller is used to clean the upper surfaces, while vertical rollers are used to clean the sides.

Modern car washes have a number of other features. For instance, many of the rollers now have limit switches. When the roller meets an object such as a mirror, the switch is tripped and the roller will slow down and move around the object. Many car washes pass cars under blowers for drying, and many also apply liquid wax after the washing cycle is complete. With water conservation becoming more important, car washes often recycle much of their water.

✦ Cash register

Ohio saloonkeeper James J. Ritty invented the modern-day cash register. Ritty was frustrated by dishonest bartenders who helped themselves to saloon profits, and he wanted a more efficient way to track sales than scribbles on scraps of paper.

While vacationing in 1879, Ritty was touring the engine room of a transatlantic steamer. He noticed a device that counted revolutions (turns) of the ship's propeller. He realized a similar device could benefit his business.

Working along with his brother John in Dayton, Ohio, Ritty developed "Ritty's Incorruptible Cash Register." This large device consisted of two rows of keys, a clocklike face with a "minute" hand to record cents, an "hour" hand to record dollars, and a bell that signaled the completion

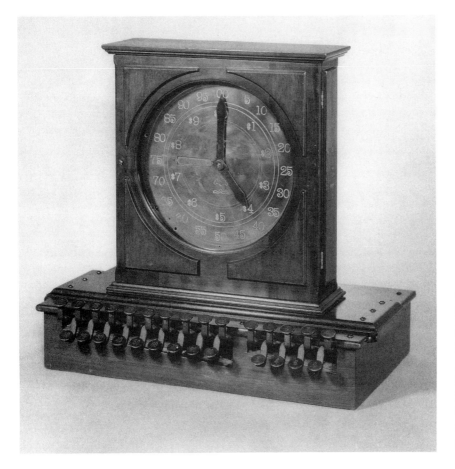

"Ritty's Incorruptible Cash Register," 1879. Ohio saloonkeeper James J. Ritty wanted a more efficient way to track sales than scribbles on scraps of paper.

of a transaction. The first model did not include any cash drawer controls or any method to maintain permanent records.

In the following years, the Ritty brothers experimented with several improved models, including one that used a paper roll to record transactions. James Ritty, unable to raise money to continue his engineering experiments, sold the company and patent for $1,000 to the National Manufacturing Company in 1881.

In 1884 the name was changed to National Cash Register Company. The new owner added an internal printing mechanism that kept a running record of sales and printed a paper sales slip. By 1910 National Cash Register monopolized the market. In 1974 the name was shortened to NCR. With the advent of electronic components and integrated circuits in the 1970s, NCR became completely electronic. The company now manufactures computers and 24-hour automated bank teller machines.

See also **Calculator, pocket; Computer, digital**

⋆ Cataract surgery

*Cataract
surgery was
mentioned in
the code of
Hammurabi,
the Babylonian
king who lived
4,000 years
ago.*

As people age, they often develop a white film over the pupil of the eye that prevents them from seeing. Cataract surgery involves removing this film, called a cataract, from the pupil or lens of an eye or removing the lens altogether and replacing it with a new lens.

Cataracts

Cataracts are spots that form on the lens of an eye, eventually clouding the lens. Cataracts interfere with vision and in extreme cases cause blindness. The lens is the part of the eye that helps the eye to focus light.

Cataracts are often associated with aging and are thus called senile cataracts. However, cataracts can be caused by diabetes, parathyroid gland abnormalities, Down's syndrome, and other conditions. Recent studies show that exposure to **ultraviolet radiation** in sunlight and artificial light during childhood may have an effect on the formation of cataracts in later life.

Types of Surgery

A surgical procedure called an introcapsular extraction involves removing the entire lens through an incision (cut) made along the top edge of the pupil. In this procedure, the lens is broken into tiny fragments that are removed from the eye. A new lens made of **plastic** is inserted and the incision is closed with tiny sutures (stitches). With the plastic lens, the patient is again able to see. The patient's vision may be further corrected with special glasses or contact lenses.

Another surgical technique, cryosurgery, freezes and destroys damaged tissue. It is successfully used to remove cataracts from the lens of the eye.

In 1979 the first **laser** eye surgery was performed. The ultra-rapid pulsated Yag laser uses bursts of controlled laser light to do surgery without having to cut the eye. Since that time laser surgery has successfully been used on corneas and detached retinas, two other common eye problems.

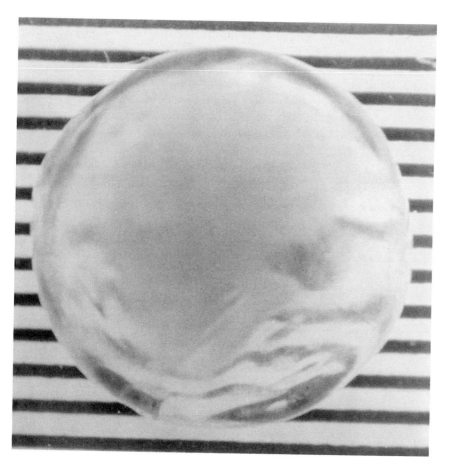

A dense cataract on a lens of an eye. Cataracts interfere with vision and in extreme cases cause blindness.

⋆⋆ Catheter, cardiac

Before the twentieth century, doctors could diagnose heart disease only by operating on a patient. This major surgery exposed the patient to much trauma and many germs. Cardiac catheterization is an effective nonsurgical means of diagnosing cardiovascular (heart) problems.

The first practical system for cardiac catheterization—passing a tube through a vein into the heart—was devised by physician Werner Forssmann (1904-1979) in 1929. Forssmann, working near Berlin, Germany, opened a vein in his own arm and inserted a catheter (a long, thin, flexible tube). Then he advanced the tube about two feet through the vein to the right side (atrium) of his heart. The position of the tube was confirmed by X-ray.

After eight more experimental procedures, Forssmann published a report describing the technique and suggesting its usefulness in examining and diagnosing diseased hearts and poor blood circulation. The procedure also provided a reliable method of determining blood flow through the lungs, blood pressure in the heart, and oxygen content of the blood, all important indications of cardiac and circulatory health.

Cardiac catheterization rapidly spread through the world and became the single most important diagnostic tool for heart disease.

⋆⋆ Cathode-ray tube

Today, almost every form of image-viewing device is based upon cathode-ray technology. This includes movie and video cameras, **televisions**, microscopes, bar-coded price scanners and **electron** guns used widely in scientific and medical applications. A cathode-ray tube is a vacuum tube in which cathode rays, usually in the form of a slender beam, are projected on a chemically treated screen and produce a luminous spot that can "scan" an electrical signal.

One cathode-ray application of particular importance has been the electron microscope, which uses a stream of electrons, rather than light, to magnify an image. These devices can even be used to magnify objects, such as ultramicroscopic **viruses** that are too small to be seen with a visible light microscope.

Cathode ray tube technology is a fairly recent invention. In the mid- to late-1800s, when the world was experiencing a scientific revolution, phenomena that had never before been truly understood, such as light, heat, and radiation, were systematically unraveled. Among these phenomena was the nature of electricity: how it worked, and why.

History of the Technology

The early experiments to solve the riddle of electricity often included the use of anode-cathode tubes—glass tubes containing an anode (an electron-collecting electrode) at one end and a cathode (an electron-emitting electrode) at the other. When most of the air was evacuated from this tube, an electrical charge could be observed jumping across the gap between the two electrodes.

One scientist who performed such an experiment was Michael Faraday (1791-1867). He noticed that as the amount of air within the tube decreased, a faint glow could be detected between the anode and the cathode. However, the technology of the time was not sufficient to produce a

Bacteria viewed through a scanning electron microscope, which uses a stream of electrons, rather than light, to magnify an image. The electron microscope is only one application of the cathode-ray tube.

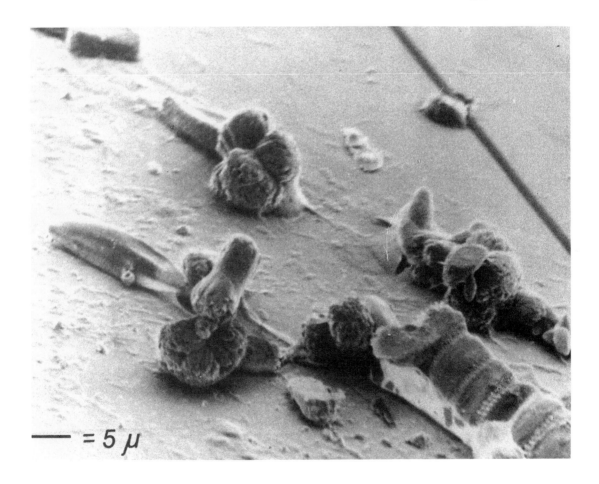

$— = 5 \mu$

high vacuum within the glass tube, and so Faraday was unable to further explore this effect.

Over the years, as many scientists tried to unlock the secrets of cathode rays, others searched for ways to apply them toward practical ends. The first such application came in 1897 in the form of German engineer Karl Ferdinand Braun's oscilloscope. This device used a cathode-ray tube to produce luminescence (light) on a chemically treated screen. The cathode rays were allowed to pass through a narrow aperture (opening), effectively focusing them into a beam which appeared on the screen as a dot. The dot was then made to "scan" across the screen according to the frequency of an incoming signal. An observer viewing the oscilloscope's screen would then see a picture of an electrical pulse.

Twentieth Century

During the first three decades of the twentieth century, inventors continued to devise uses for cathode-ray technology. Inspired by Braun's oscilloscope, A. A. Campbell-Swinton suggested that a cathode ray tube could be used to project a video image upon a screen. Unfortunately, the technology of the time was unable to match Campbell-Swinton's vision.

It was not until 1922 that Philo T. Farnsworth used a magnet to focus a stream of electrons onto a screen, producing a crude image. Though the first of its kind, Farnsworth's invention was quickly superseded by Vladimir Zworykin's kinescope, the ancestor of the modern television.

⋆⋆ Cell

A cell is the basic unit of life.

A cell is the basic unit of life. It is the smallest part of living organisms capable of surviving independently and reproducing itself. Every living organism is made of cells, but the size and shape of the cells varies according to their function.

All cells, however, have the same basic structure. The protoplasm—the living substance that makes up the cell—consists of two main parts: the nucleus and the cytoplasm.

Nucleus

The nucleus is a round body near the center of the cell that contains the hereditary material determining the cell's structure and activities. Heredity refers to the passing on of characteristics from one generation to the next.

This material, called chromatin, ordinarily looks like a ball of tangled string, but begins to turn into rodlike **chromosomes** during cell division.

These chromosomes contain packages of **DNA** (**deoxyribonucleic acid**), the information that essentially acts as a blueprint for the human body. The cell nucleus also contains nucleoli, which contain proteins and **RNA** (**ribonucleic acid**).

Cytoplasm

The cytoplasm is responsible for keeping the cell alive. It is made up mostly of water, but contains tiny organelles that each have a job keeping the cell alive. For instance, some organelles give the cell power to

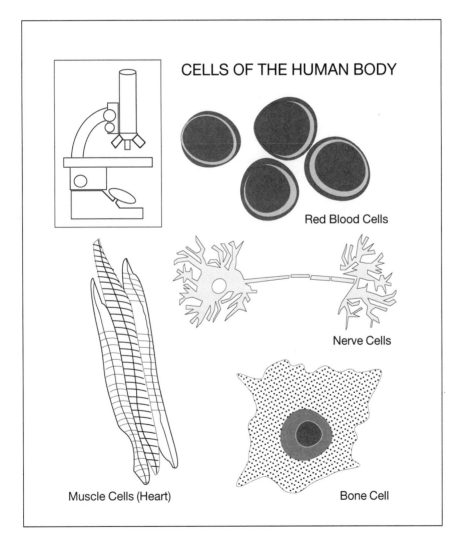

CELLS OF THE HUMAN BODY

Red Blood Cells

Nerve Cells

Muscle Cells (Heart)

Bone Cell

Every living organism is made of cells, but the size and shape of the cells varies according to their function.

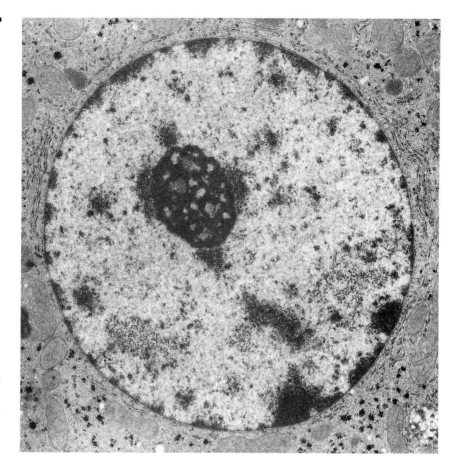

Nucleus of a rat's liver cell. A cell is the smallest part of living organisms capable of surviving independently and reproducing itself.

move, others break down dead cells, some manufacture proteins for cell growth, and still others help with cell reproduction.

By 1882 German botanist Eduard Strasburger (1844-1912) had recognized that protoplasm had important components. He invented the terms "nucleoplasm" to describe the protoplasm within the cell nucleus and "cytoplasm" for the protoplasm outside the nucleus.

⋆⋆ Chemical warfare

Throughout history people have used chemicals in warfare. Ancient armies burned painted wood to create smoke screens or to force enemies from hiding places. The Spartans of ancient Greece used sulfur dioxide against their rivals, the Athenians, during the Peloponnesian War in 429 B.C. by burning pitch and sulfur on wood to create poisonous sulfur smoke near an enemy city. The Byzantines were able to destroy enemy ships by using Greek fire, a chemical mixture that burst into flames when it came into contact with water. During the Middle Ages (A.D. 400-1450), a group of Christians saved Belgrade (in eastern Europe) from advancing Turks by dipping rags in poison, lighting them, and fanning the fumes at the enemy.

World War I

Chemical warfare was put to greater use during World War I (1914-18). When England set up a naval blockade that prevented Germany from importing nitrates to use in manufacturing explosives, Germany turned to its chemical industry.

German chemists created a way to use chlorine to form a gas cloud that would blow onto the Allied (English, French, and United States) front lines. The German army introduced this weapon on April 22, 1915, by

Four U.S. C-123 aircraft spraying a dense enemy jungle position with Agent Orange, a defoliant the military used to burn the leaves off plants and destroy possible enemy hiding places.

releasing 160 tons of liquid chlorine from nearly 6,000 pressurized cylinders over Ypres, Belgium. The Allied soldiers were totally unprepared, and the casualties were horrendous: 5,000 dead and 10,000 injured.

Both sides worked on developing better delivery systems, which included putting the gas into tubes in **artillery** shells. The Germans also created mustard gas, which produced severe blisters on all body surfaces. In addition, mustard gas remained on the ground and equipment where it could cause injuries long after the original attack. Mustard gas was so vicious that there was no way to effectively defend against it.

Mustard gas remained on the ground and equipment where it could cause injuries long after the original attack.

World War II

During World War II (1939-45), newer and more powerful chemicals were created for use on battlefields. The Germans created the first of the nerve gases. When inhaled or absorbed through the skin, nerve gases killed their victims in minutes, while mustard gas took hours. But the German

A soldier in a gas mask and protective suit applies anti-gas cream.

military never did use nerve gas during the war. Why? Because they mistakenly assumed that the Allies had access to such weapons and would use them in retaliation.

Cold War

After World War II, the Cold War between the Soviet bloc and the United States necessitated the development of deadlier chemical weapons. The United States developed and used Agent Orange, a defoliant, in the Vietnam War to destroy enemy hiding places in forests and jungles. Today, chemical weapons are popular with many smaller nations that cannot support nuclear weapons research and development.

See also **Gas mask**

⋆⋆ Chemotherapy

Chemotherapy is the treatment of a disease or condition with chemicals. Today the term is most often associated with the treatment of cancer. Chemotherapy drugs include the sulfonamide drugs developed in the 1930s, **penicillin** and other **antibiotics** of the 1940s, the **hormones** of the 1950s, and the more recent drugs that interfere with cancer cell growth.

Genetically engineered cancer vaccines are now being tested against several virus-related cancers, including liver, cervix, and nose and throat cancers.

Bacterial Infections

For thousands of years, medical practitioners have used plants and other substances to treat symptoms of disease. The challenge was to find the right drug to seek out and destroy infectious organisms within the body without harming healthy **tissues**. In 1910 German physician Paul Ehrlich discovered that an arsenic compound was successful in treating the sexually transmitted disease **syphilis**. (For a complete discussion of antibacterial drugs, see **Antibiotics**.)

Viral Infections

The first effective chemotherapeutic agent against **viruses** was acyclovir. It was produced in the early 1950s by the American biochemists George Hitchings and Gertrude Belle Elion for the treatment of herpes. Today's antiviral drugs are being used to combat influenza (flu) and **AIDS** via the AIDS treatment drug AZT, which inhibits the reproduction of the human immunodeficiency virus (HIV).

Cancer Treatment

Scientists began trying various chemical compounds for use as cancer treatments as early as the mid-nineteenth century. But the first effective treatments were the sex hormones, first used in 1945—estrogens for prostate cancer and both estrogens and androgens to treat breast cancer. In the next 20 years, scientists developed a series of useful antineoplastic (anti-cancer) drugs; in 1954 the forerunner of the National Cancer Institute was established in Bethesda, Maryland.

Today drugs are used alone, in combination, and along with radiation and/or surgery. The success rate varies depending on the type of cancer and whether it is localized (in one spot) or has spread to other parts of the body. Drugs are also used after treatment to keep the cancer from reappearing. Since many of the drugs have severe side effects, their value must always be weighed against the serious short- and long-term effects, particularly in children, whose bodies are still growing and developing.

Plant alkaloids have long been used as medicines, such as colchicine from the autumn crocus. Cancer therapy drugs include vincristine and vinblastine, derived from the pink periwinkle. They prevent mitosis (division) in cancer cells. The most recently tested drug is taxol, derived from the bark of several species of yew trees. Discovered in 1978, taxol was undergoing clinical trials in 1993.

Another class of naturally occurring substances are anthracyclines, which scientists consider to be extremely useful against breast, lung, thyroid, stomach, and other cancers.

Certain antibiotics are also effective against cancer cells and are now used against cancer of female reproductive organs, brain tumors, and other cancers.

Genetically engineered cancer vaccines are now being tested against several virus-related cancers, including liver, cervix, and nose and throat cancers.

⋆⋆⋆ Chewing gum

People have been chewing naturally gummy substances since earliest times. The ancient Greeks chewed resin from the mastic tree, while the Maya of Central America chewed chicle, the latex sap of the wild sapodilla

How Gum Is Made

Workers slit the bark of chicle-producing trees and collect in cups the latex that runs out. The small quantities are later combined, boiled, and formed into blocks for shipment. At the chewing gum factory, the chicle is ground, melted, and purified. After sweeteners and flavors are added, the gum is rolled into balls or flattened and sliced into the sticks we find in stores.

tree. The North American Indians chewed spruce tree sap and taught the New England colonists to do the same. In the mid-1800s, sweetened paraffin (candle wax) replaced spruce resin as the preferred substance for chewing gum.

Chewing Gum Goes Commercial

Chicle, the base for chewing gum, is thought to have been brought to the United States by the Mexican general Antonio López de Santa Anna (1794-1876) in the 1860s. When he returned to Mexico, the general left a chunk of chicle behind with an acquaintance, inventor Thomas Adams, Sr.

Adams experimented with uses for the chicle. While it did not make a good rubber substitute, Adams found that it did make an excellent chewing gum. The inventor set up a Jersey City factory and began marketing his tasteless "Adams' New York Gum—Snapping and Stretching." This was soon followed by licorice-flavored Black Jack.

Salesman Thomas Adams, Jr., promoted the gum, and sales and the number of competitors soon grew. More flavors were added to chewing gum, which was soon sold in vending machines. William Wrigley, Jr. (1861-1932) made his gum the world's most advertised product. He began by giving away sticks of "chewing candy" to promote sales of his father's baking powder.

Bubble gum was first produced in the early 1900s by Frank Fleer of the Fleer Company. Called Blibber-Blubber, it was unsatisfactorily wet and sticky. Fleer's much-improved Dubble Bubble Gum appeared in 1928 and was an instant success. Frank's brother, Henry, came up with the candy-coated chicle tablets that the Fleers named Chiclets.

Chicle remained the basic ingredient of chewing gum until World War II (1939-45). Wartime shortages spurred the development of synthetic

Bubble gum was first produced in the early 1900s by Frank Fleer of the Fleer Company. Called Blibber-Blubber, it was unsatisfactorily wet and sticky.

gum and plastic substitutes for chicle. Sugarfree gum came on the market in the mid-1960s.

✦ Chocolate

Chocolate originated in the New World, a product of cacao beans grown by the Maya and Aztec Indians of Central America before the arrival of Christopher Columbus (1451-1506). From the cacao bean, they made a bitter but stimulating drink called *xocoatl*, which was served cold. The Aztec emperor Moctezuma consumed 50 golden goblets of this brew a day.

Europe Likes Chocolate

The Spanish conquistador Hernando Cortés (1485-1547) and his troops were served *xocoatl* shortly after their arrival in Mexico in 1519. When they returned to Spain, they brought cacao beans and the bitter drink back with them. (Columbus had introduced cacao beans to the Spanish royal court in 1502, but no one had been interested.) In Spain, the drink was sweetened, flavored with vanilla and cinnamon, and served hot.

The Swiss made the first chocolate bar in 1819.

The recipe for drinking chocolate was a closely guarded secret of the Spanish for almost 100 years. Around 1606, an Italian traveler managed to bring knowledge of chocolate to his country, and the drink became all the rage in France following the marriage in 1659 of Princess Maria Theresa of Spain (1638-1683) and King Louis XIV (1638-1715).

England was introduced to the beverage in 1657, when a Frenchman opened a chocolate shop in London. Similar shops spread through Europe and became fashionable meeting spots for the wealthy. In England, the drink remained a beverage of the well-to-do until the high import duty on cacao beans was lowered in the mid-1800s.

The Swiss made the first chocolate bar in 1819. Nearly ten years later, a Dutchman devised a press to create chocolate powder. Finally, in 1875, Daniel Peter of Switzerland added condensed milk and sugar to chocolate, inventing milk chocolate.

How Chocolate Is Made

After cacao beans are scooped out of their melon-like fruit, they are fermented and dried. They are then cleaned, roasted, hulled, and broken into pieces. When ground, the cacao beans release their natural fat, called cocoa butter. Together the cocoa butter and finely ground beans—a liquid mixture—are known as chocolate liquor, from which all chocolate products are made.

Ruth Wakefield's chocolate chip cookie became so popular that Nestlé officials wondered why sales of its semisweet bars had become so high in the Boston area.

Chocolate Returns to the New World

The first chocolate factory in the United States was established in 1765 in Dorchester, Massachusetts, financed by James Baker, whose Baker's chocolate became an American standard. Another American institution, the Hershey Chocolate Company, was founded in 1900 after Milton S. Hershey (1857-1945) sold his caramel factory and turned to the manufacture of chocolate instead. Hershey built a complete model town named after himself in southeastern Pennsylvania. Today Hershey is known for its chocolate-based amusement park.

Inventing the Chocolate Chip Cookie

Perhaps the best-known use of chocolate is the chocolate chip cookie, an accidental invention by Ruth Wakefield. Wakefield was the proprietor of the Toll House Inn in Whitman, Massachusetts.

One day in 1933 Wakefield was in a hurry to make Butter Drop-Do's. Instead of taking the time to melt squares of chocolate, she decided to break a semisweet chocolate candy bar into pieces and add it to the batter, assuming the chocolate would melt during baking. Instead, to Wakefield's surprise, the bits of chocolate remained intact.

Wakefield's new "chocolate crunch cookies," later renamed "Toll House cookies," were a hit with her customers. After the recipe was published in a Boston newspaper, the cookie became so popular that Nestlé officials wondered why sales of its semisweet bars had become so high in the Boston area. When Nestlé found the reason, it began to manufacture the bars with score lines so they would break more easily, and invented a chopper to cut the chocolate into the right-sized pieces.

Between 1939 and 1940, Nestlé began selling chocolate morsels, ready to be mixed into the cookie dough, and bought the Toll House name and cookie recipe from Wakefield. Ever since, the Original Nestlé Toll House cookie recipe has appeared on the back of the morsels wrapper.

✦ Cholera

Cholera epidemic occurred in Peru when government officials changed the chlorination procedures in the public water system. Without enough chlorine present, the cholera bacteria flourished.

Cholera epidemics are bred in areas where poor sanitary conditions exist, particularly crowded urban settings. An epidemic is when many people in the same area have a disease at the same time. Cholera epidemics have been reported since ancient times.

Cholera is an often fatal disease. Despite advances in medicine, cholera outbreaks still occur today. The 1991 epidemic in South America and the 1994 epidemic among Rwandan refugees in Africa are reminders that technology has not yet conquered this dangerous disease.

Cholera is caused by the comma-shaped *Vibrio cholerae* **bacteria**, which attack the intestines. Cholera is a highly contagious disease spread primarily by unwashed hands, unwashed fruit, and water contaminated by sewage. A cholera victim's first symptoms are diarrhea, vomiting, and cramps. Eventually, the body loses too much liquid and dehydration sets in. Then the victim's face takes on a bluish tint and the arms and legs become dark and cold as blood circulation slows.

About one to three days after exposure to the cholera bacteria, diarrhea sets in. Diarrhea is the frequent elimination of loose or liquid stools. Uncontrolled diarrhea leads to dehydration (loss of body fluids). Cholera victims are treated with large amounts of fluids and glucose (sugar) shots to build up strength. This type of rehydration therapy is less effective during severe outbreaks when health facilities are overcrowded with victims. Rehydration therapy has, nevertheless, saved countless lives.

Battling Cholera

The cholera bacteria was isolated by Robert Koch, a famous germ theory pioneer. A German physician, Koch, led a government-supported scientific expedition into Egypt where a cholera epidemic was underway in 1883. The epidemic ended before Koch had completed his research. So he took his group to India, where another cholera epidemic was underway. He completed his research there. Researchers are at work on an oral (pill form) vaccine that could prove to be effective.

Today, public water systems in industrialized nations have water treatment plants. These plants rely on chemicals such as chlorine to keep bacteria growth under control. The current cholera vaccine is not recommended to Americans traveling abroad, since the brief coverage it offers does not offset its side effects.

⋆⋆ Cholesterol

Cholesterol is one of the most common steroids and is found in almost all animal body **tissues**, particularly the nervous system, liver, kidneys, and skin. It forms part of **cell** membranes.

The buildup of cholesterol in arteries has long been linked to increased risk of heart disease. However, the body does have a use for cholesterol—in the right amounts. The body uses cholesterol as the basis for synthesizing (making) **vitamin** D, **cortisone**, adrenal gland **hormones**, and sex hormones.

The body's cholesterol level is regulated by low-density lipoprotein (LDL)-receptors, which pass cholesterol and LDLs into the cell for use. When there are more LDL molecules than LDL-receptor molecules, the LDL accumulates in the blood. It is currently believed that a related substance, high-density lipoprotein (HDL), carries cholesterol out of the tissues.

For several decades scientists have associated cholesterol with the buildup of damaging plaque in the arteries (atherosclerosis), which can cause heart attacks. Health authorities have urged people to eat foods very low in animal fats, including cholesterol, to improve their health.

However, research published in 1992 associates low cholesterol levels (below 160 mg per 100 ml blood serum) with a variety of diseases. Another study strongly supports an earlier hypothesis that LDL is important in the buildup of plaque in the arteries only when the blood contains high levels of iron. Research continues in order to understand cholesterol's precise role in human health and disease.

Research continues in order to understand cholesterol's precise role in human health and disease.

⋆⋆ Chromosome

Chromosomes are thread-like bodies in the cell nucleus of all plants and animals that hold the **genes**—the blueprints of **heredity**. Each chromosome carries a single strand of **DNA** (**deoxyribonucleic acid**) that threads together about 1,000 genes.

The connection between chromosomes and heredity was not made until 1902.

Early scientists learned about tiny organisms such as cells by coloring them and placing them under a microscope. Some parts of the cell would absorb more dye and their outlines would be clearer.

Not much was known about chromosomes prior to the 1880s due to the lack of adequate cell staining (coloring) techniques and poor microscopes. In 1879, however, German anatomist Walther Flemming (1843-1905) used new synthetic dyes and was able to see objects that had previously gone undetected in cells. He noticed that some material scattered throughout the nucleus heavily absorbed the dye and coined the word "chromatin" to describe this dark stainable substance.

Upon further observation, Flemming noted that when a cell divided into two daughter cells, the chromatin doubled and then split lengthwise, leaving each daughter cell with the same amount of chromatin as the parent cell. By 1882 Flemming had identified all the stages of this process, a basic operation of cell division now termed "mitosis."

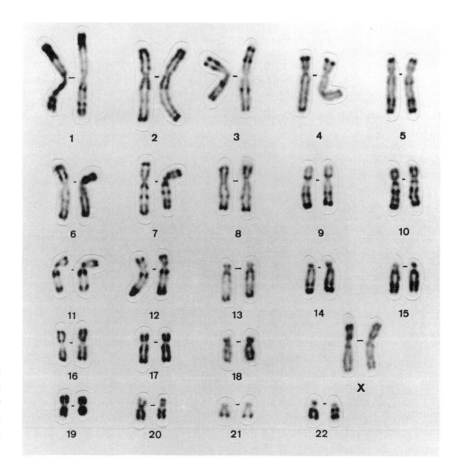

1 2 3 4 5

6 7 8 9 10

11 12 13 14 15

16 17 18 X

19 20 21 22

Healthy female chromosomes. One or more hereditary traits is linked to specific chromosomes.

The Heredity Connection

In 1888 the German anatomist Wilhelm von Waldeyer-Hartz renamed Flemming's chromatin "chromosomes," meaning "colored bodies." However, the connection between chromosomes and heredity was not made until 1902 when American geneticist Walter S. Sutton (1877-1916) published a short scientific article concerning the newly discovered work of Gregor Mendel. This nineteenth-century Austrian monk was an early student of genetics, or the study of how traits pass from one generation to the next. Sutton proposed that the "factors" that Mendel could not identify but believed controlled heredity were indeed contained in the chromosomes. German zoologist Theodor Boveri independently came to a very similar conclusion, and in 1903 their work became known as the chromosomal theory of inheritance.

For many scientists, the theories of Mendel and Sutton provided a sufficient explanation for heredity and evolution. However, the American geneticist Thomas Hunt Morgan (1866-1945) tested their theories using the fruit fly as his subject. The results of his experiments and those of his assistant Hermann Muller contributed greatly to the understanding of chromosomes and their role in heredity.

Morgan found that genes—the term Wilhelm Johannsen coined for Mendel's "factors"—were located on chromosomes. For the first time, it was clear that one or more hereditary traits was linked to specific chromosomes. Morgan also discovered that genes on the same chromosome were often inherited together. However, chromosome pairs would sometimes break apart and exchange pieces—a process known as crossing over.

The findings of Morgan and his colleagues focused the attention of the scientific world on chromosomes and prompted further research in the area of genetics.

See also **Sex chromosome**

⋆⋆⋆ Clock and watch

In the early days of humanity, only three divisions of time existed: days, months, and years. The first artificial division of time was the hour, probably established by the Egyptians during the fourth millennium B.C. Beginning at dawn and dusk, 12 hours each were given to night and day.

Unfortunately, the changing seasons cause the length of night and day to vary by several hours. Thus the Egyptian hour was not really a fixed unit.

In winter, for example, because nights are longer than days, 12 night "hours" would last longer than 12 day "hours."

What was needed was a device that could measure time in regular, unvarying amounts. So early scientists began work that would lead to the modern clock.

Early Clocks Track the Sun

Ancient observers noticed that as the sun traveled across the sky, shadows on the ground would move and vary in size. This led to the invention of the sundial. The first sundial was probably a simple stick in the ground. Later the Egyptians built large obelisks, which work on essentially the same principle.

When properly read, sundials served as a fairly accurate method for marking the passage of time. However, they proved to be difficult for many to interpret.

Other Early Clocks

The first mechanical timekeeping device was a water clock called a clepsydra. It operated by pouring a steady stream of water into a vessel.

A sundial. When properly read, sundials serve as a fairly accurate method for marking the passage of time. Sunlight falls on a vertical pole placed at the center of a standard dial, casting a shadow on the dial.

After a certain period the vessel would fill, then tip itself empty, and be ready for refilling. The amount of time this took could be regulated by changing the size of the vessel. Water clocks were used from about 1500 B.C. through the Middle Ages (A.D. 400-1450).

There were many problems with water clocks. Depending upon the climate, the water in the clock would often evaporate, causing the device to lose time, or freeze solid, stopping the machine entirely.

During the Middle Ages the two professionals most skilled in the construction of clocks were astronomers and monks. Astronomers used the devices to plot the motions of the heavens. Monks needed them to know when to toll the monastery bell. A monk probably invented the first completely mechanical clock around A.D. 1275.

As the accuracy of timepieces increased, society came to certain realizations about the nature of the world. First, it became apparent that days (that is, daylight hours) varied in length throughout the year. Second, it was found that the sun did not rise at the same time all over the world. This latter phenomenon was not addressed until 1884, when the world adopted Greenwich Mean Time, giving us **time zones**.

The next step in the evolution of the clock was the development of improved escapements, which are mechanical devices that ensure regular motion within the clock. Near the beginning of the fifteenth century, engineers were using coiled springs in door locks and handguns. Borrowing from this technology, clockmakers developed the first spring-driven clocks around 1430.

Even with the addition of springs, clocks before the mid-1600s were notoriously inaccurate. About that time, history tells us, the Italian astronomer **Galileo Galilei** was in the Tower of Pisa during an earthquake. As the ground shook, Galileo watched the motion of swinging chandeliers with fascination. By timing their swing against his own pulse, Galileo found that the amount of time it took a chandelier to swing from one side to another was constant, no matter what the distance. This was the inspiration for the pendulum clock.

During this same time scientists became occupied with a new puzzle—inventing a timekeeping device that could be used aboard sailing ships for navigation. Because of the motion of the waves at sea, both weight-driven and pendulum clocks were unsuitable. In 1674 Dutch astronomer Christiaan Huygens introduced a watch that featured a balance spring as a regulator, acting in place of a pendulum. In 1761 a balance

Historians believe the Chinese and Egyptians invented the sundial independent of each other and thousands of miles distant.

spring was joined with a mainspring-driven clock to create a precise and completely portable watch, suitable for ships as well as a person's wrist.

The common wristwatch is among the most precise mechanical instruments. If a watch loses 20 seconds every day it is still operating at an error rate of only 0.023 percent—all the more remarkable since it is expected to run 24 hours a day, 365 days a year, a task required of no other measuring device. Still, clockmakers at the turn of the twentieth century were not yet satisfied.

Electric Clocks

Clocks powered by electricity had been in existence since the late 1800s, but most required large and ungainly machinery in order to function. These early battery clocks used tiny motors to wind the mainspring when it ran down.

The real revolution in battery-operated timepieces came during the 1950s when the Swiss put a tiny electric tuning fork inside a watch. When the battery applies a small charge to the tuning fork, it will vibrate continuously at a very specific rate. That vibration can be used in place of a clock's slowly unwinding mainspring.

Since the invention of the Swiss-movement watch, most tuning forks have been replaced with tiny pieces of quartz crystal, a natural substance that can vibrate with much greater precision than any artificial substance. Even the most affordable quartz clock is accurate to within one minute per year.

Today the **atomic clock** is used as a reference standard for absolute time. First constructed in 1948, the atomic clock measures the unvarying frequencies at which molecules vibrate. By knowing how many times a molecule will vibrate within a unit of time, the atomic clock can be used to regulate the accuracy of other clocks. Such absolute precision is essential for navigation, particularly in space, as well as research on the atomic level. Watches set by atomic clocks will lose less than one second every 1,000 years.

⋆*⋆ Cloning

The phenomenon of identical twins has always attracted attention. After an egg is fertilized, it begins to divide repeatedly. If the egg completely separates during the two-cell stage, identical twins will result. Both individuals will have exactly the same combination of **genes** (genotype) and each will have the same physical characteristics (phenotype). This is an

Opposite page: A replica of the clock built by Giovanni dé Dondi in the fourteenth century. As the accuracy of timepieces increased, society came to certain realizations about the nature of the world.

Cloning technology has enabled breeders to develop lines of cattle, sheep, and cotton plants that respectively produce more milk, wool, and cotton.

What Is a Clone?

A clone is a group of genetically identical **cells** descended from a single common ancestor. Science has capitalized on the mechanisms of cellular reproduction to produce clones. Advances in biotechnology since the 1970s have enabled livestock breeders to clone virtually unlimited numbers of identical animals from a single embryo, allowing the precise duplication of an animal with desired characteristics.

In 1979 veterinarian Steen Willadsen developed a way to divide sheep embryos in half at the two-cell stage, making clones possible. In the next few years, several scientists made further strides in this area with both sheep and cattle embryos. A team developed a simplified method of dividing and cloning sheep embryos in 1984.

example of how exact duplicates can naturally occur through sexual reproduction. Cloning is an artificial way of producing twins.

As an example of cloning techniques, dairy farmers trying to clone a cow with high milk-producing qualities begin by artificially inseminating a high-producing cow with the sperm from a prize bull. The resulting embryo, which contains the entire genetic instructions needed to form a complete calf, develops within its mother. After some time, the embryo divides into a mass of 32 identical cells. The embryo is then carefully removed from the mother cow and separated into 32 separate cells. Finally, after microsurgery on the cells, each new embryo is transplanted into 32 different carrier cows, where it develops fully.

After a normal pregnancy, each carrier cow gives birth to a calf that is genetically identical to the 31 other calves derived from the original 32 cell embryo. Each calf is a clone. The trait for increased milk production has been cloned so that the farmer now has 32 high milk-producing cows instead of just one. Cloning technology has enabled breeders to develop lines of cattle, sheep, and cotton plants that respectively produce more milk, wool, and cotton.

Cloning is one area of genetics that is advancing very rapidly, and it is therefore not without controversy. If this technology is ever applied to humans, who will decide which genes are "desired" and should be cloned? This is only one of many important questions that have arisen as a result of the amazing advances in genetic cloning.

See also **Animal breeding**

⋆⋆ Clothes dryer

The development of the clothes dryer followed that of the **washing machine**. An early design was patented by the African American inventor G. T. Sampson in 1892.

The first successful home drying machines were designed in the 1930s by J. Ross Moore. Moore sold his designs to the Hamilton Manufacturing Company of Two Rivers, Wisconsin, who then called in industrial designer Brooks Stevens to help redesign the machine. It was Stevens who came up with the idea for the window in the dryer's door so consumers would know what the machine was for. Stevens advised Hamilton to display the window-doored dryer in stores with a pair of "boxer shorts flying around in there."

Hamilton made the only dryers marketed in the United States before World War II (1939-45). They were simple machines that operated at fixed temperatures. Modern dryer improvements began in 1960 with Maytag's introduction of electronics. Today's dryers have automatic cycles with varying temperatures and can shut themselves off when the clothes reach the correct stage of dryness.

⋆⋆ Cocaine

For centuries, Peruvian (South American) natives have chewed the leaves of the coca plant because of their stimulating and exhilarating effect. Albert Niemann studied the white powder made from the leaves and named it "cocaine" around 1859, noting also the temporary numbing effect the compound had on his tongue.

During the 1880s in Vienna, Austria, the great psychologist Sigmund Freud (1856-1939) studied cocaine as a treatment for **morphine** addiction. Morphine was used as a pain killer. Freud also suggested the possible use of cocaine as a local anesthetic to a Viennese colleague, Carl Koller (1857-1944), a young ophthalmologist. Koller experimented on animals and then presented his findings to the Congress of Ophthalmology in Heidelberg, Germany, in 1884, demonstrating the successful use of cocaine as a local anesthetic during eye surgery.

American doctor William Halsted soon followed up on Koller's work by experimenting with cocaine injection into nerves to produce local **anes-**

For many years, the addictive properties of cocaine went unrecognized.

The widespread use of cocaine and the resulting increase in violence associated with drug dealing was an important factor in stimulating the "war on drugs" in the United States that has continued since the 1980s.

thesia. By the end of 1885, Halsted had performed more than 1,000 operations using cocaine as an anesthetic. Unfortunately, Halsted also discovered another of cocaine's properties: he became addicted to the substance and spent many years overcoming his dependence.

Harvey Cushing (1869-1939), a student of Halsted's, coined the term "regional anesthesia" for this use of cocaine, in contrast to the "general anesthesia" produced by ether. Ether puts the entire body to sleep while cocaine and other regional or local anesthetics numb only a portion of it. Later in 1885, Leonard Corning (1855-1923), a New York neurologist, injected a cocaine solution as a spinal anesthesia.

For many years, the addictive properties of cocaine went unrecognized. As a pain reliever and stimulant, the drug was a common ingredient in the very popular patent medicines of the late 1800s and early 1900s. Doctors freely prescribed cocaine for any number of ailments. Once the addictive dangers became known, scientists concentrated on developing synthetic (manufactured) substitutes for the anesthetic properties of cocaine. One of the first of these was **Novocain**.

Today cocaine is only occasionally used medically, sometimes as a local anesthetic for some kinds of surgery. Most cocaine now is purchased and used illegally. Cocaine is often inhaled ("snorted"), sometimes injected, and as free base is smoked. The most potent form of cocaine, crack, is also smoked. The widespread use of cocaine and the resulting increase in violence associated with drug dealing was an important factor in stimulating the "war on drugs" in the United States that has continued since the 1980s. Today cocaine is distributed by the Medellín cartel (group) of Colombia and reaches the United States and other sites by boat, plane, and human carriers.

⋆⋆ Color photography

When black and white photographs became common, photographers and subjects alike began to call for full-color photographs.

The late 1850s saw the development of what would become the standard method of color **photography**: the additive three-color process. With this process, three distinct negatives were taken through color filters. These filters—red, green, and blue-violet—could be positioned over each other to create an image with a full range of color.

The late nineteenth century saw the introduction of a light-sensitive emulsion (gel) to a glass plate on the side opposite to the camera lens. The mirror effect that resulted created a multi colored group of light rays. Although practical drawbacks limited the application of his discovery and limited commercial success, inventor Gabriel Lippmann was awarded the Nobel Prize in physics in 1908 for having devised the first direct process of color photography.

Professional and Amateur Photographers

Employing the conventional additive three-color process, the American inventor Frederic Eugene Ives first made color photography practical for professional photographers. With his 1893 Photochromoscope camera, three "separation" negatives were taken in succession—using the red, green, and blue-violet filters—onto a single photographic plate. The professional photographer could use a customized viewing machine developed by Ives to get a positive color image.

The French inventors and manufacturers Auguste and Louis Lumiere developed the first method of color photography accessible to amateurs. Their image consisted of small flecks of color, which blended visually to create an effect like that of an impressionistic painting.

In 1912 the German scientist Hans Fischer made a definite breakthrough by proposing that color photography could be achieved chemically. Although Fischer's own attempts to devise a color film failed, his concept is the basis for modern color film.

Eastman-Kodak Gets Involved

In 1935 Leopold Godowsky and Leopold Mannes, both professional musicians, declared their invention of a practical color film that used the oxidizing process proposed by Fischer. Godowsky and Mannes ultimately worked with the American photographic inventor George Eastman, the founder of Eastman-Kodak, who marketed the film as Kodachrome.

Within a few years, various companies had achieved Fischer's goal of incorporating color-forming chemicals into the emulsion layers of the film itself. These first color films produced transparencies, and the procedures for satisfactorily transferring a color photograph onto paper were gradually perfected.

In 1963 the American founder of the Polaroid Company, Edwin Herbert Land, marketed a product that made Fischer's goal seem modest. This was polacolor, a color film for the **instant camera** that produced photographs instantly and automatically. With this innovation, the century-old goal of achieving color photography had clearly been reached.

⋆⋆ Color spectrum

White light, being a composite, is made up of many different colors.

The spectrum of sunlight is a familiar sight, particularly after a rainstorm when tiny particles of water suspended in the air will split the **Sun**'s white light into a rainbow. In physics, a spectrum is a group of items that are always ordered in the same way. The light spectrum always appears as red,

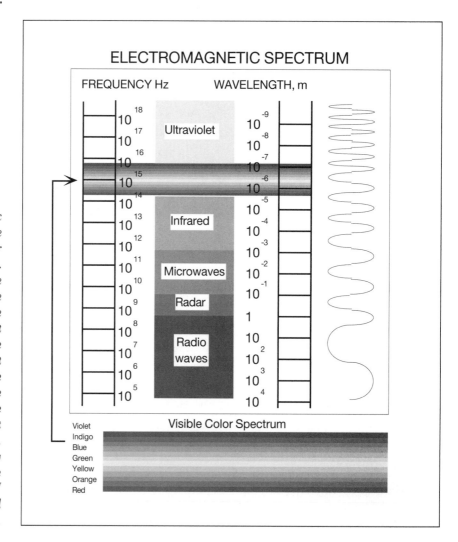

ELECTROMAGNETIC SPECTRUM

Visible Color Spectrum

Violet
Indigo
Blue
Green
Yellow
Orange
Red

The electromagnetic spectrum and the visible color spectrum. The light we can see with the naked eye is called "visible light." Visible light is made up of the color spectrum. But on either side of the visible light scale are light waves we cannot see without special instruments. However, we know they exist and make use of them for TV broadcasting and medical diagnosis.

orange, yellow, green, blue, indigo (blue), and then violet. Anyone who has played with a prism has probably duplicated this phenomenon.

The first person to examine the color spectrum in this way was the renowned English physicist and mathematician Sir **Isaac Newton** (1642-1727), and it was he who provided the first insight into the composite (made of parts) nature of light.

Newton Experiments

Newton performed his optical experiments between 1665 and 1666. First Newton obtained a beam of light by allowing sunlight to pass through a small hole in a curtain. He then directed that beam through a prism and onto a screen. Expecting a broad circle of white light, Newton was quite surprised to see instead a narrow band of colors.

At first, Newton assumed that the colors were caused by the prism glass. However, when the color spectrum was passed through a second prism it was recombined into a beam of white light. Also, Newton found that light of a single color could not be further dispersed—that is, a beam of red light passed through a prism would not be split into a "red spectrum."

As light enters a prism each color is bent to a different degree. This causes the light to spread out, forming the spectrum.

Newton correctly presumed that the spectrum was a property of or belonged to the light itself. White light, being a composite, is made up of many different colors. As it enters the prism it is bent slightly. More importantly, each color is bent to a different degree from the rest. This causes the light to spread out, forming the dispersion (widespread) spectrum.

It is now known that light acts in many ways as a waveform, with many different wavelengths. Longer wavelengths are always bent more sharply than shorter wavelengths. This is why the color spectrum of white light is always arranged—in order of decreasing wavelengths—red, orange, yellow, green, blue, indigo, and violet. This order is often remembered using the phrase "ROY G BIV."

Producing the Color Spectrum

In addition to prisms, there are other methods for obtaining the spectrum of light. Early scientists would shine light through a narrow aperture (hole). This would cause the light to bend outward slightly, producing a small spectrum. By constructing a wire mesh called a diffraction grating, a much wider and more sharply defined spectrum could be produced. More modern diffraction gratings are constructed by marking the surface of optically flat glass.

As scientists studied the spectra of sunlight, candlelight, and starlight, they began to notice tiny dark lines crossing the colored bands. By calculating the positions of these lines, they were able to determine the elements that were contained in the light's source.

The science of examining spectra and spectral lines is called **spectroscopy**. In addition to visible light, spectroscopy also examines the spectra of infrared radiation, **ultraviolet radiation**, and **X-ray** radiation.

See also **Light, diffraction of; Light, theories of; Wave motion, law of**

The color spectrum of white light is always arranged—in order of decreasing wavelengths— red, orange, yellow, green, blue, indigo, and violet. This order is often remembered using the phrase "ROY G BIV."

⁎⁎ Combustion

Combustion is usually associated with fire. In fact, fire was the first chemical reaction that people discovered how to create and control more than one million years ago. When a fuel (such as wood) combines with **oxygen** in the air, the fuel burns, giving off heat and light, or flames.

Besides using fire for cooking, prehistoric people learned to use it to harden clay into pottery, produce metal from ores found in the ground, and melt metals together to make new materials such as bronze. Because fire was capable of bringing about such dramatic changes, the ancient Greeks and early chemists (called alchemists) considered fire to be one of the four basic elements of nature from which all other things are made.

Then during the 1600s, scientists began to recognize the potential of a new source of power—steam, which is produced from water by the heat given off during combustion. In addition to the importance of fire in every-day life, this new interest in steam made the combustion process a popular subject of scientific study.

During the 1700's, chemists began to realize that measuring the quantity of substances involved in a combustion reaction is critical to understanding that chemical reaction. The idea of quantitative measurement, pioneered by the Italian astronomer **Galileo Galilei** (1564-1642), had been spreading slowly from the science of physics to chemistry. **Isaac Newton**'s (1642-1727) highly successful physical experiments eventually convinced chemists to begin making quantitative measurements, too. By the late eighteenth century, they had learned that combustion changes the weight and volume of the substances involved, and French chemist L. B. Guyton de Morveau (1737-1816) had demonstrated that metals gain weight during combustion.

Meanwhile, scientists had also begun to suspect that air contains individual gases, each with its own characteristics. During the 1770s, after **carbon dioxide** and **hydrogen** had been discovered, two chemists, Joseph Priestly and Carl Wilhelm Scheele, independently identified a new gas that greatly promotes the combustion process. Scheele called it "fire air" because substances require the gas in order to burn.

It was the great chemist Antoine-Laurent Lavoisier (1743-1794) who finally put all these pieces together. Although Lavoisier repeated the work of several earlier chemists, he alone grasped the truth of the combustion process. Burning materials were combining with a portion of the air, which increased their weight. Lavoisier realized that the gas discovered by Scheele and Priestley—which he renamed "oxygen"—was precisely the same as that part of the air that reacts with substances during combustion.

By the early 1800s, the chemical changes associated with combustion had become well understood. Since then scientists have focused on specific mechanisms of the process, such as flame propagation (multiplication). Besides the familiar visible flame, combustion includes any chem-

People first used combustion to light campsites and cook food. Later, combustion would drive locomotives and fuel factories.

ical reaction that gives off heat (for example, the burning of gasoline inside a car engine).

Sometimes materials such as oily rags or bales of hay can burst into flame without a spark to start the fire. This dangerous phenomenon, called spontaneous combustion, occurs when the heat produced naturally within the substance cannot escape. In some combustion reactions, other chemicals such as chlorine or **fluorine** take oxygen's place as the "oxidizer" in the combustion process.

⋆⋆ Comic strip and comic book

*Early
adventure
strips included
"Superman,"
"Tarzan,"
"Terry and the
Pirates," and
"Prince
Valiant."*

Early Attempts

The late 1800s and early 1900s saw the rise of the comic strip, a series of drawings that tell a story. England's W. F. Thomas created one of the first regularly featured characters, Ally Sloper, who appeared from 1884 to 1920. In the United States Richard F. Outcault (1863-1928) created "Hogan's Alley" (later renamed "The Yellow Kid") in 1895. This popular strip starred Mickey Dugan, a kind of aged baby dressed in a trademark yellow sack with printed comments. Originally published in the *New York World,* it also appeared in the *New York Journal* and spurred a tug-of-war between the two newspapers, giving rise to the term "yellow journalism."

In 1897 Rudolph Dirks's (1877-1968) "Katzenjammer Kids," based on an earlier cartoon called "Max und Moritz" by Wilhelm Busch (1832-1908), appeared in the *New York Journal.* The year 1907 brought readers the first successful daily comic strip, Bud Fisher's "Mr. Mutt" (later "Mutt and Jeff") drawn for the *San Francisco Chronicle.*

Adventure Tales

By the 1930s, adventure strips had gained popularity in the United States, among them "Dick Tracy," created by Chester Gould (1900-1985). This strip featured a square-jawed police detective who tangled with creatively named, odd-looking villains.

*Opposite page:
Superman was one
of the first of
dozens of comic
superheroes that
included Batman,
Captain America,
and Wonder Woman.*

Other early adventure strips included "Superman," "Tarzan," "Terry and the Pirates," and "Prince Valiant." Comic strips today include offerings such as "Mary Worth," featuring a middle-aged, motherly adviser, and "Peanuts," a creation of Charles Schulz (1922-). The dog Snoopy and the

Happy Birthday Big Gun —

round-headed Charlie Brown have helped make Schulz's strip one of the most successful.

Serial Concerns

Beginning in 1924 with "Little Orphan Annie" by Harold Gray (1894-1968), comic strips have often blended entertainment with social commentary or political satire. Early examples include "Li'l Abner," originated in 1934 by Al Capp (1909-1979), and "Pogo" in 1949, by Walt Kelly (1913-1973). Today "Doonesbury," by Garry Trudeau, chronicles the progress of its college-friend characters from the turbulent era of the 1960s through the present. "Outland" and its predecessor "Bloom County," by Berke Breathed, use animal and human characters to comment on society.

Booklet Format

The first comic book was an 1897 collection of reprints of the "Yellow Kid" strip. A collection of "Mutt and Jeff" reprints appeared in 1911, while Japan published the first comic book featuring original material in 1920. Comic books became especially popular during World War II (1939-45), providing welcome entertainment for soldiers stationed away from home.

The rise of television in the late 1940s diverted public attention from comic books, but their popularity rose in the 1960s, and they still attract readers and collectors.

⋆⋆ Communications satellite

So many satellites have been launched that an unexpected problem has arisen— crowding of the synchronous orbit.

Before 1956, people could only speak to each other across the Atlantic Ocean by radiotelephone. If atmospheric (weather) conditions were poor, the connection was poor. Then in 1956, the first transatlantic **telephone cable** went into operation, providing 36 static-free telephone circuits. The cable was laid along the ocean floor. By the early 1960s, there were still only about 40 channels of transatlantic communication, with little promise that the ocean-bottom cables could handle future demand.

Early Visions

As early as 1945, Arthur C. Clarke, a British science fiction writer, had described the possibility of establishing a communications network covering the entire globe using just three strategically orbiting satellites. The technology needed to realize the vision was some time in coming. The challenges were many:

- A **satellite** would be exposed to extreme conditions of heat and cold.
- The satellite would need an independent power supply to last for months or years.
- Once in orbit, the satellite could be reached only by **radio** signal, so it would have to be able to operate independently.
- Finally, rocket science was in its infancy, and launching a satellite into orbit posed serious problems.

In 1957 the Soviet Union's *Sputnik 1* was the first artificial satellite to be launched. In 1958 the United States established a satellite connection between New Jersey and California using the moon as a reflecting sur-

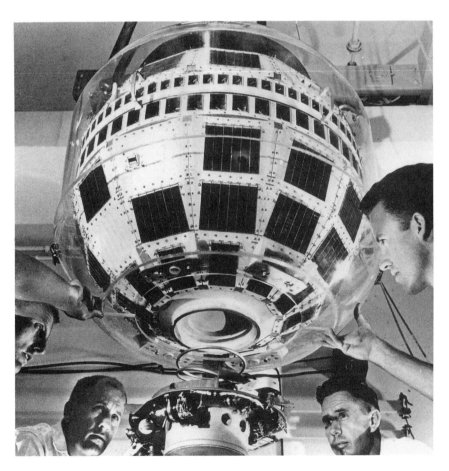

In July 1962, AT&T paid NASA to launch Telstar 1, the first transatlantic relay satellite. Douglas Aircraft technicians are shown mating the experimental satellite to the third stage of a Delta rocket.

face for radio signals. In July 1962, AT&T paid NASA (the National Aeronautics and Space Administration) to launch *Telstar 1,* the first transatlantic relay satellite. It was in operation until February 1963 and transmitted telephone calls, facsimiles, and **television** broadcasts between ground stations in Maine, England, and France.

These early satellites orbited around the earth at low and medium altitudes and moved in and out of range of the fixed ground stations. The *Syncom* series of satellites, developed by Hughes Aircraft, was the first to be launched into high altitude, geosynchronous orbit. This means they rotate through space along with Earth, always remaining in the same position relative to Earth. Thus they can stay in continuous contact with the ground stations.

Besides equipment for communications, early satellites carried cameras for meteorological (weather) and other scientific observation. Mete-

*Syncom 4 was one
of the first satellites
to always remain in
the same position
relative to Earth.*

orological satellite pictures are now widely used by television weather forecasters.

Space Gets Crowded

Since the 1960's, so many satellites have been launched that an unexpected problem has arisen—crowding of the synchronous orbit. The United States and Canada, for instance, are competing for the same spots in the synchronous orbit for their domestic communications satellites.

Recent developments in **fiber optics**, which have greatly enhanced the capacity of telephone and television cables, may mean a shift back to ocean-bottom cable for many communications needs. However, the many different applications of satellite technology, such as observation, ensure that satellites will circle Earth for a long time to come.

⋆⋆ Compact disc player

The 1980s saw a major step forward in the reproduction of sound. High quality compact discs (CDs) rapidly replaced long playing vinyl (LP) records and have steadily gained on the cassette tape market. Music lovers appreciate the compact disc's ability to offer clear, distinct instrument sounds without distracting background noise. The secret is digital recordings done from the original. The technology is a relatively recent discovery.

One of the first Sony compact disc players available to consumers. High quality compact discs rapidly replaced LP records and have steadily gained on the cassette tape market.

Technology Developments

Once the conditions required to store information digitally were understood, devices capable of carrying out such storage had to be invented.

The introduction of the **laser** in 1960 by Theodore Maiman would make the compact disc player a reality. Engineers at a number of audio firms realized that a laser beam could be used to retrieve digital data from a recording without physically touching it, and set about developing a practical **optical disc**. A number of digital recording and playing systems came out of this effort.

The Philips and Sony corporations began a joint effort to create a standard, superior digital playback system that they could license to any other company wishing to produce a CD player. Within about a year, they had succeeded, and beginning in the early 1980s, CD players came onto the market in earnest.

How Compact Disc Players Work

The system adopted by Sony and Philips works as follows: digital impulses coded from music, pictures, or voice are embossed as peaks and valleys on a hard plastic disc. The plastic is coated with a thin microscopic layer of metal such as **gold** or aluminum. The metal is then coated with a resinous protective layer. The finished disc, called a CD (compact disc), is about 4.7 inches (12 cm) in diameter.

In a compact disc player, a small laser beam shines upon the peaks and valleys on the metalized portion of the disc while the disc spins. A mirror or prism between the laser and the disc picks up light reflected from the disc and bounces it onto a photosensitive diode, which transduces the impulses into electrical current. The current is then converted into an analog waveform for playback through stereo speakers.

Evidence suggests that Arab sailors were using compasses as early as A.D. 600.

⋆⋆ Compass

The compass is a tool used by land and sea explorers to help them know where they are and in which direction they are going. Before compasses were developed, people used the sun, wind, and stars as their guides. The compass allowed them to calculate their location and direction with greater accuracy.

During the first century B.C., the Chinese observed that pieces of lodestone, an iron mineral, always pointed north when they were placed on a surface. This discovery led to the development of the compass. The first Chinese compass was a spoon made of lodestone that rested on a smooth surface with markings indicating the four directions. The next step in the advancement of compasses was to enclose the lodestone in a decorative casing with a needle to indicate which direction was north.

One problem compass makers encountered was that the iron they used for the pointer lost its magnetism easily. This was a problem because without the magnetic attraction, the needle did not move. After experimenting with different metals, the Chinese combined **carbon** and **iron** to make steel. The steel was stronger than iron and held its magnetic charge for a long time.

Meanwhile, other navigators around the world were also discovering the compass. Evidence suggests that Arab sailors were using compasses as early as A.D. 600. As Arabs spread their influence into North Africa, Spain, and France, they brought with them an extensive knowledge of the most advanced sailing and navigation techniques known at the time. Thus, the compass was introduced to Europe.

By the fourteenth century, European ships carried maps on which were charted compass readings to reach different destinations. These charts used a symbol to indicate directions of north, south, east, and west with each quarter of the symbol divided into 90 degrees.

During the fifteenth century, Prince Henry of Portugal (1394-1460) had a great influence on the development of sailing and navigation. He established a school for navigators in Portugal, and encouraged sailors and mapmakers to coordinate their information to make more accurate maps of the seas. One of his innovations was to set the compass inside brass rings connected to each other and attach it to a stand, which allowed the compass to remain level even when the ship swayed in rough waters.

Another of the innovations that came in the fifteenth century was the discovery of magnetic declination. When Christopher Columbus (1451-1506) sailed from Spain to the New World, he noticed that his compass did not align

Without a compass, Christopher Columbus might not have found the New World.

directly with the North Star. The difference between magnetic north and true north was called declination.

In 1581 an English navigator named Robert Norman hypothesized that the earth had magnetic fields that run parallel to its surface. He made diagrams of these fields and explained the difference between the geographical axis of Earth and its magnetic axis. Charts similar to his still appear on modern maps. Norman's diagrams made it possible for navigators to determine the magnetic declination for any given position on the map, thus their calculations were much more accurate than ever before.

Further improvements were made to maps and compasses when it was discovered that declination was affected not only by location but by time. Over a period of years, **Earth's magnetic field** shifts, changing the declination for any given place.

Prince Henry of Portugal had a great influence on the development of sailing and navigation. One of his innovations allowed a ship's compass to remain level even when the ship swayed in rough waters.

As maps and ships improved, new compasses and new problems developed. In 1789 a British doctor, Gowin Knight, rubbed a bundle of magnets on an iron bar to create super magnets, which in turn magnetized compass needles for longer periods of time. A great success, Knight's super magnets were used by the British navy for over 80 years.

However, by 1850 all ships in the British navy contained iron, which interfered with the magnetism of the compass and led to false readings. British physicist William Thomson, Lord Kelvin corrected this by using small corrector magnets that surrounded the compass and prevented deviation.

An American, Elmer Sperry, built the first gyrocompass, a device that worked day or night, anywhere on Earth, even at the poles where lines of force are too close together for magnetic uses to function properly.

By 1935 many pilots used gyrocompasses because they were steady in all types of weather and they never spun wildly even in the sharpest turns. The U.S. **submarine** *Nautilus* used a gyrocompass when it crossed under the North Pole because the gyrocompass was not affected by the powerful magnetic forces there.

Rockets depend on gyrocompasses because in space magnetic poles cannot influence the needles on traditional compasses.

⋆⋆ Computer, analog

A digital **computer** performs calculations based strictly upon numbers or symbols. The analog computer, on the other hand, translates always changing quantities (such as temperature, pressure, weight, or speed) into corresponding voltages or gear movements.

The analog computer then performs "calculations" by comparing, adding, or subtracting voltages or gear motions in various ways. The final result of the calculation is sent to an output device such as a **cathode-ray tube** or pen plotter on a roll of paper. Common devices such as thermostats and bathroom scales are actually simple analog computers: they "compute" one thing by measuring another; they do not count.

Analog computers are still used today for some applications such as scientific calculation, engineering design, industrial process control, and spacecraft navigation.

Early Examples

The earliest known analog computer is an **astrolabe**, built in Greece during the first century B.C. Using gears and scales, the astrolabe predicted the motions of the sun, planets, and stars.

Other early measuring devices were also analog computers. Sundials traced a shadow's path to show the time of day. Springweight scales, which have been used for centuries, convert the pull on a stretched spring to numbers or pounds.

In 1905 Rollin Harris and E. G. Fisher of the U.S. Coast and Geodetic Survey started work on a calculating device that would forecast tides. Called the "Great Brass Brain," it contained a maze of cams, gears, and rotating shafts. It made accurate predictions and was used for 56 years before being retired in 1966.

The Modern Age

Vannevar Bush, an electrical engineer at the Massachusetts Institute of Technology (MIT) in Cambridge, created what is considered to be the first modern computer in the 1930s. He and a team from MIT's electrical engineering staff, discouraged by the time-consuming mathematical computations required to solve certain engineering problems, began work on a device to solve these problems automatically.

In 1935 the incredible second version of their device, called the "differential analyzer," was unveiled. It weighed 100 tons, and contained 150 motors and hundreds of miles of wires connecting relays and vacuum tubes. Three of the machines were built for military and research use. Over the next 15 years, MIT built several new versions of the computer. By present standards the machine was slow, only about 100 times faster than a human operator using a desk calculator.

In the 1950s, RCA produced the first reliable design for a fully electronic analog computer. By this time, however, many of the most complex functions of analog computers were being assumed by faster and more accurate **digital computers.** Analog computers are still used today for some applications such as scientific calculation, engineering design, industrial process control, and spacecraft navigation.

⋆⋆⋆ Computer application

Applications are computer programs that allow a person to use data in different ways. Databases, spreadsheets, word processing, page layout pro-

A student being introduced to a computer. Applications are computer programs that allow a person to use data in different ways. For example, databases, spreadsheets, word processing, page layout programs, and drawing programs are all computer applications.

grams, and drawing programs all are electronic versions of older "paper" business systems. Some applications include their own languages, allowing the user to write related routines or customize use of the application.

Applications were written for **mainframe computer** systems beginning in the 1950s. The wide variety of user-oriented applications began with the personal computer, beginning in the mid-1970s, developing along with faster processing chips, larger computer memory and disk storage, and more flexible operating systems.

The modern software industry began in 1975, when William Gates and Paul Allen wrote an interpreted version of the language BASIC for the first personal computer, the Altair. This made it easy and even fun to write applications. As other computers were invented, Gates licensed versions of BASIC to run on them as well. By the mid-1980s, Gates's company, Microsoft, had become the leading software publisher and he was a billionaire.

Besides Microsoft, other prominent software companies are Lotus Development Corp., founded by Mitchell Kapor, Novell Inc., founded by Ray Noorda, Borland International Inc., headed by Philippe Kahn, and WordPerfect Corp.

Database Management Systems

A database is an electronic version of a set of index cards. A database management system allows the user to find specific words and names, to sort the records by specific fields, such as last name or zip code, and otherwise specify which information is presented and how it is displayed. Programs exist for single desktop computers, mainframes, and **computer networks.** Databases are now being designed to include illustrations, video, and music and other sounds, as well as words and numbers.

Word Processing

Word processing programs begin with the basic features of a typewriter and add abilities available only with a computer: quickly moving text from one position to another (cutting and pasting), producing individually addressed copies of the same letter (mail merge), checking spelling, and replacing one word or phrase with another throughout a document (global search and replace).

The first word processors, such as those produced in the 1970s by Wang Laboratories, were not computers. Their sole purpose was word processing. The first popular word processing software for personal comput-

The modern software industry began in 1975, when William Gates and Paul Allen wrote an interpreted version of the language BASIC for the first personal computer, the Altair. By the mid-1980s, Gates's company, Microsoft, had become the leading software publisher and he was a billionaire.

ers was WordStar, published by Micro Pro in 1978. Today the most widely used programs are WordPerfect (WordPerfect Corp.) and Microsoft Word, both dating from the early 1980s.

Many word processing programs also provide features for professional-quality desktop publishing, such as page design and layout and insertion of illustrations. The finished product is printed on a high-resolution laser printer. There are also specialized page layout programs, such as PageMaker (Aldus Corp.) and Ventura Publisher (Xerox).

Spreadsheets

Spreadsheets are electronic versions of the traditional accounting spreadsheet written on columnar paper. Like the paper version, an electronic spreadsheet categorizes information in columns and rows.

Spreadsheets are also used to see future values in "what if" situations, such as increasing sales or opening a new factory. Today's spreadsheets

A computer-aided design (CAD) of gas turbines. When combined with a database of parts, specifications, and costs, someone with a computer can design a new product and can also specify the materials and the product's expected performance.

can also provide charts and other visualization of the data. Accounting programs are spreadsheets that are already formatted for business management, such as payrolls, inventories, accounts payable, and accounts receivable.

Graphics

Computerized graphics programs perform the jobs that used to be the work of drafters and graphic artists. Two-dimensional programs are used for line drawings or for black-and-white or color paintings. Popular software includes Coral Draw (Corel), Harvard Graphics (Software Publishing Co.), and PC Paintbrush (ZSoft).

Three-dimensional figures, both outlined (or wire) and solid, are also available with some graphics programs. These are often used by industry as CAD/CAM (computer-aided design/computer-aided manufacturing). When combined with a database of parts, specifications, and costs, someone with a computer can design a new product and can also specify the materials and the product's expected performance. AutoCAD (AutoDesk) is a widely used example.

Graphics programs also make possible the games played on computers, game systems, and arcade game machines. They are the basis for many educational applications.

Communications

Communications programs allow computers to communicate with each other either over telephone lines by modem or over the direct cabling of computer networks. Transferring files, sending and receiving data, using data stored on another computer, and electronic mail (e-mail) systems that allow people to receive messages in their own "mailboxes" are some common uses of communications software.

A network operating system, such as NetWare (Novell Inc.) and Lantastic (Artisoft), handles the basic functions of network communications, such as directing data to the correct computer address and maintaining the flow of data.

Networking has led to the formation of workgroups, in which people work together by using the same computer programs rather than by being in the same place physically. Workgroup management programs include Lotus Notes (Lotus Development Corp.) and Windows for Workgroup (Microsoft).

Graphics programs make possible the games played on computers.

⋆⋆ Computer, digital

The digital computer is a programmable electronic device that processes numbers and words accurately and at enormous speed. It comes in a variety of shapes and sizes, ranging from the familiar desktop **microcomputer** to the minicomputer, **mainframe**, and **supercomputer**. The supercomputer is the most powerful in this list and is used by organizations such as NASA (National Aeronautics and Space Administration) to process upwards of 100 million instructions per second.

The impact of the digital computer on society has been tremendous. In its various forms, it is used to run everything from spacecraft to factories, health care systems to telecommunications, banks to household budgets.

The story of how the digital computer evolved is largely the story of an unending search for labor-saving devices. Its roots go back beyond the calculating machines of the 1600s to the pebbles (in Latin, *calculi*) that the merchants of Rome used for counting, to the abacus of the fifth century B.C. Although none of these early devices was automatic, they were use-

Part of Intel's supercomputer being installed at the California Institute of Technology (Cal Tech) in Pasadena on May 30, 1991. It was world's fastest computer to date.

ful in a world where mathematical calculations performed by human beings were full of human error.

Counting Machines

By the early 1800s, with the Industrial Revolution well underway, errors in mathematical data had assumed new importance. Faulty navigational tables, for example, were the cause of frequent shipwrecks. Such errors were also a source of irritation to Charles Babbage, a brilliant young English mathematician. Convinced that a machine could do mathematical calculations faster and more accurately than humans, Babbage in 1822 produced a small working model of his Difference Engine. The machine's arithmetic functioning was limited, but it could compile and print mathematical tables with no more human intervention needed than a hand to turn the handles at the top of the model.

The first digital computer, the Mark I was composed of 78 calculators and adding machines linked together.

Babbage's next invention, the Analytical Engine, had all the essential parts of the modern computer: an input device, a memory, a central processing unit, and a printer.

Although the Analytical Engine has gone down in history as the prototype of the modern computer, a full-scale version was never built. Even if the Analytical Engine had been built, it would have been powered by a steam engine, and given its purely mechanical components, its computing speed would not have been great. Less than 20 years after Babbage's death in 1871, an American by the name of Herman Hollerith was able to make use of a new technology—electricity—when he submitted to the United States government a plan for a machine that would be used to compute 1890 census data. Hollerith went on to found the company that ultimately emerged as IBM.

Modern Versions Are Room Size

World War II (1939-45) was the motivation for the next significant stage in the evolution of the digital computer. Out of it came three mammoth computers. The Colossus, a special-purpose electronic computer, was built by the British to decipher German codes. The Mark I was a gigantic electromechanical device constructed at Harvard University under the direction of Howard Aiken. The ENIAC, a fully electronic machine, was much faster than the Mark I.

The ENIAC operated on some 18,000 vacuum tubes. If its electronic components had been laid side by side two inches apart, they would have covered a football field. The computer could be instructed to change programs, and the programs themselves could even be written to interact with each other. For coding, Hungarian-born American mathematician John von Neumann proposed using the **binary** numbering system—0 and 1—rather than the 0 to 9 of the **decimal system**. Because 0 and 1 correspond to the on or off states of electric current, computer design was greatly simplified.

Since the ENIAC, advances in programming languages and electronics—among them, the transistor, the integrated circuit, and the microprocessor—have brought about computing power in the forms we know today, ranging from the supercomputer to far more compact models.

Mark I Is Built

When Mark I was completed in January 1943 it was moved to Harvard, where it performed its first calculations in May 1944. The machine was used for different military calculations during its 15-year life.

See also **Computer, analog**

The ENIAC operated on some 18,000 vacuum tubes. If its electronic components had been laid side by side two inches apart, they would have covered a football field.

Charles Babbage, English Inventor

Charles Babbage (1791-1871) was born in the early years of the Industrial Revolution, the time when mankind began its love affair with machines. However, Babbage held extreme views on what these labor-saving devices could do for industry and commerce, and most of his colleagues regarded him as a crank. Today he is remembered as the brilliant mathematician who invented the prototype (first version) of the digital computer in use today.

Babbage entered Cambridge University at the age of 19, and it was there he first thought of a computer. The idea of a machine that seemed to perform human thought processes struck many of his colleagues as ridiculous, if not sacrilegious. One evening in 1812, as he sat gazing at a table of mathematical data, it occurred to him that a machine could calculate such data faster than humans and without human error. He devoted his life to building such a machine.

Babbage never did see numbers calculated by a steam-powered machine. But he did complete a small working model of the Difference Engine in 1822. This machine could compile and print mathematical tables. The next year, he began building a full-scale version. Progress was slow and expensive, since machine tools for making the parts had to be custom crafted.

His next project was the Analytical Engine. A programmable automatic machine, the Analytical Engine was the direct ancestor of the modern digital computer. It would have been far simpler for Babbage to implement his ideas with electromechanical devices than with mechanical ones, but it would be many years before electrical technology was reliable enough for Babbage's purposes.

Babbage tossed off ideas and designs for other devices with great abandon—among them, a cowcatcher for locomotives, a meter to reduce water waste, a device for recording earthquake shocks, and a skeleton key. He also designed an ophthalmoscope, a multipurpose machine tool, and a lighthouse signaling system.

Had Babbage been born a few generations later, when technology was more advanced, the world might not have had to wait until the mid-twentieth century for the digital computer.

Howard H. Aiken, American Computer Scientist

Howard H. Aiken (1900-1973) designed and built the Automatic Sequence Control Calculator (ASCC), the first digital computer in the United States to work from a program and produce reliable results. The machine was also called Mark I.

In 1923 Aiken received a bachelor's degree in electrical engineering from the University of Wisconsin. After working as an industrial engineer, he entered graduate school at Harvard University. He earned a master's degree in 1937 and a Ph.D. in physics in 1939. He then joined the Harvard faculty, becoming a full professor in 1946.

While in graduate school, Aiken began to design a machine to speed up the calculating of differential equations (a complicated kind of math). He based it on the Analytical Engine designed by the English computer pioneer Charles Babbage (1792-1871). Several calculating machine manufacturers and even the president of Harvard refused to consider Aiken's design. Finally in 1939 IBM's president, Thomas J. Watson, agreed to build it. Construction continued during World War II (1939-45), while Aiken was a navy commander and then head of the navy's computing project.

Mark I Is Built

Mark I was an electromechanical calculator and used both electronics and a mechanical system to work its calculations. Mark I was composed of 78 calculators and adding machines linked together. It could perform arithmetic and look up data (information) on tables. Operations were controlled by punched paper tape. The operator input information from punched cards or tape or from hand-set switches. Mark I gave back output that was punched on cards or printed on paper.

Aiken built more advanced versions, called Mark II, Mark III, and Mark IV. In January 1947 he became head of Harvard's new Computation Laboratory. People in this laboratory were pioneers in advanced computer research, inventing natural languages, computer commands and processing, computer circuit theory, data processing, and magnetic storage devices.

After retiring from Harvard in 1961, Aiken became Distinguished Professor of Information Technology at the University of Miami in Florida.

✦ Computer disk and tape

The first commercial computers used punched cards and paper tape to store information. During the late 1940s, however, computer engineers began to explore other ways to store information because the cards and paper were bulky, prone to damage, and difficult to access. When **magnetic recording** technology emerged after World War II (1939-45), computer designers were quick to see the possibilities such a technology could offer them.

Plastic Storage Tapes

In 1949 J. Presper Eckert and John Mauchly introduced BINAC (Binary Automatic Computer), the first computer to employ magnetic tape for storage. The **plastic**-based tape it used was able to hold far more information per unit size than punched cards.

BINAC, however, was merely a stripped-down forerunner of a more advanced machine called UNIVAC (Universal Automatic Computer), completed by Eckert and Mauchly two years later. UNIVAC replaced BINAC's plastic tape with a stronger metal tape. Once better plastics were developed, however, they returned to use as they were safer and caused less wear to tape-reading components.

Tapes, however, were still not fast enough for computers that could perform thousands of calculations per second, so other proposals were advanced. For a time, rapidly rotating magnetic drums were used as a storage medium, but drums could not be engineered to meet the need for greater speed of access that emerged as computers continued to improve.

Reynold Johnson, an engineer at IBM, inspired by the work of Russian-born American inventor Jacob Rabinow, began work on the concept of using spinning disks as a data storage method in 1952. By 1955 he and his staff had developed a massive hard disk unit, which consisted of a set of 50 platters, each two feet wide, coated with a magnetic material and mounted on spindles rotating 1,200 times per minute. A read/write head moved back and forth between disks to obtain information. Later models added separate heads for each disk. Called "jukeboxes," the machines were quite effective despite their bulk.

Floppy Disks Introduced

The development of the floppy disk followed the hard disk drive of the 1950s. The floppy was able to hold less data than the hard disk and it was slower in operation. But the 8-inch plastic floppy, devised in the late 1960s, had two advantages over the hard disk drive system: portability and less susceptibility to damage. These advantages rapidly made floppy disks a mainstay in computing and floppy disks were included with personal computers (PCs) when they came on the market in 1981. Newer floppy disks are much smaller (common are the 5.25 inch and 3.5 inch sizes) and can hold far more data—up to 1.44 megabytes (1.44 million bytes, equivalent to 720 typed pages of information).

Hard Drive Debuts

The success of personal **microcomputers** led to further innovations. Once again, the need of users for more data storage outstripped the capacity of floppy disks. In the early 1980s, a team of IBM engineers headed by Philip D. Estridge was assigned the task of improving the IBM-PC by adding a better storage system. Estridge and his team developed the fixed

Eight, 5.25, and 3.5 inch floppy disks. Portability and less susceptibility to damage rapidly made floppy disks a mainstay in computing.

hard drive, a unit mounted permanently within the chassis (body) of the computer and coated with a magnetic material. It was capable of holding 30 times the data of the early floppy disks—10 megabytes (5,000 pages) of information.

The hard drive, in fact, made so much information available to the user at once that IBM had to modify its PC design to accommodate the disk. First, a new **computer operating system** capable of handling and organizing large numbers of files was introduced. In addition, the computer was given the ability to "boot" or load its operating system directly from the hard disk when the computer is turned on. This means that a user no longer needed to insert a series of floppy disks when switching the computer on.

In the late 1980s, Plus Development of California introduced a Hard-Card, which contains a fixed disk that fits directly into the expansion slots of IBM's personal computers for those who wish to add a hard drive. Small hard disk drives are available for laptop computers as well. In 1987 IBM came out with a new 3.5 inch hard disk capable of holding the equivalent of over 120 megabytes (60,000 pages of data). In the late 1980s, a new medium called the **optical disc** was introduced. Systems such as CD-ROM and WORM surpassed the floppies and hard disks in performance by delivering portability, reliability, greater storage capacity, and lower cost.

See also **Computer, digital**

⋆ Computer, industrial uses of

Computers in industry are drastically changing the way products are made and profoundly changing the jobs of the people who make them.

CAD/CAM

In 1947 the California Institute of Technology in Pasadena devised a method for using computers to aid in designing **aircraft**. By 1950 the Massachusetts Institute of Technology (MIT) in Cambridge had developed an automatically controlled milling machine used in cutting metal parts. In 1963 Sketchpad, an early forerunner of the computer-aided design (CAD) system, was developed by Lincoln Laboratories. A similar system, DAC-1 from General Motors, was developed at the same time.

In 1968 MIT and the U.S. Air Force jointly developed a CAD/CAM (computer aided manufacturing) system to drive lathes (metal cutting

Implementing labor-saving ideas involving the computer, particularly for industrial and mechanical purposes, is a never-ending process.

Computer-aided design (CAD) of an aerospace hydraulic system. Using interactive graphics workstations, designers, engineers, and architects can create models or drawings, increase or decrease sizes, rotate or change them at will, and see results instantly on screen.

machines) and tooling machines used in the aeronautics (aircraft) industry. By the 1970s, a number of new methods were developed to remove much of the boring manual processes from design and manufacturing work.

Now an essential part of industry, CAD/CAM, as it is more commonly called, is the process of using the computer in design and manufacturing functions. Thousands or tens of thousands of highly technical and accurate drawings and charts are required for the many design specifications, blueprints, material lists, and other documents used to build complex machines. If the engineers decide structural components need to be changed, all the plans and drawings must also be changed.

Prior to CAD/CAM, human designers and drafters had to change them manually, a time-consuming and error-prone process. When a CAD system is used, the computer can automatically evaluate and change all corresponding documents instantly. Using interactive graphics workstations, designers, engineers, and architects can create models or drawings, increase or decrease sizes, rotate or change them at will, and see results instantly on screen.

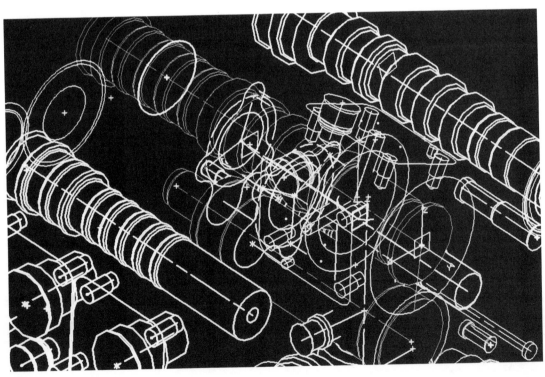

Computer Simulation

CAD use is particularly valuable in space programs, where many unknown design variables are involved. Previously, engineers depended upon trial-and-error testing and modification, a time-consuming and possibly life-threatening process. However, when aided by **computer simulation** and testing, a great deal of time, money, and possibly lives can be saved. Besides its use in the military, CAD is also used in civil aeronautics and in the automotive and data processing industries.

CAM, commonly utilized in conjunction with CAD, uses the computer to communicate instructions to automated machinery. CAM techniques are especially suited for manufacturing plants, where tasks are repetitive, tedious, or dangerous for human workers. The use of CAD/CAM systems enables the production of better, less expensive products.

Computer integrated manufacturing

Computer Integrated Manufacturing (CIM), a term popularized by Joseph Harrington in 1975, is also known as Autofacturing. CIM is a programmable manufacturing method designed to link CAD, CAM, industrial **robotics**, and machine manufacturing using unattended processing workstations. CIM offers person-free, uninterrupted operation from raw materials to finished product, with the added benefits of quality assurance and automated assembly.

CAE (computer-aided engineering), which appeared in the late 1970s, combines software, hardware, graphics, automated analysis, simulated operation, and physical testing to improve accuracy, effectiveness, and productivity. The use of computers has greatly expanded industry's ability to produce high-quality affordable products. For example, complex machines such as videocassette recorders (VCRs) and **microwave ovens** are readily available to the average consumer, in part because of computer-assisted manufacturing.

But industry's reliance on computers has led to two new problems. First, many manufacturing employees have worked with mechanical machines all their lives and are hesitant about learning new electronic systems. Second, those very efficient electronic systems have reduced the need for many manufacturing workers, who must be retrained for new jobs.

See also **Computer application; Computer input and output devices; Computer vision; Cybernetics**

⋆⋆ Computer
input and output devices

When computers were introduced into wide usage after World War II (1939-45), they revolutionized the way modern societies function. Primarily, they have allowed for the more efficient processing and storing of vast amounts of information. The material processed by a computer, however, must still be entered into its data banks in some way, and must be output to be used. The development of "user friendly" devices to enter and extract information has been essential to the computer's success because these are the parts of a computer system with which most people regularly interact.

Early Efforts

Many methods of input have been developed, each presenting certain advantages and disadvantages. Punched cards were the first output devices used by modern computer designers. They were bulky to store, carried limited data, and could be easily damaged.

The modem was one of the first input devices to help create worldwide linking capabilities among computer systems. The word "modem" is an acronym for MODulator/DEModulator, which describes the process of changing digital (computer) signals to analog (telephone) signals and vice versa. Modems came into use in the 1950s and allowed computers to hook up to each other through telephone lines. But modems tied up telephone lines and did not always work well.

Magnetic tape, developed and used during the late 1950s, is now used more as a storage medium than an input method.

The terminal was first introduced as an input device in the mid 1960s. It was known by several names (such as VDTs—video display terminals, and CRTs—**cathode-ray tubes**). The terminal usually consisted of a keyboard and display screen. Keyboards produce letters by using codes and electronic signals to represent characters. The method is time consuming and hurt by electrical power failures.

The light pen, introduced in 1963, makes contact with the screen and light-sensitive cells in the pen tip transmit an electronic signal, allowing users to write or modify on-screen images. Touch-sensitive monitors work in a similar manner except the user simply touches the appropriate place on the monitor rather than using a light pen.

Digitizing tablets, invented by the RAND Corporation in 1964, allow a graphic image to be scanned, converted into digital data, and displayed or revised on screen. These systems are widely used in graphics, engineering, and design work.

Specialized point-of-sale (POS) terminals began appearing in retail outlets in 1973. POS terminals perform typical **cash register** functions, but also track inventory, transmit data, and check credit inquiries. Often paired with optical scanners or wand readers, POS terminals have helped decrease operating costs for many retailers.

Newer Devices

A mouse or "pet" peripheral, is a fairly new input device, first included with the Apple Computer Corporation's LISA microcomputer in 1983. It contains a rolling ball and a panel with one or more buttons. When it is rolled on a smooth, flat surface, several small, light-sensing diodes

Using an electronic sketch pad, a technician adds color to a computer-generated animated figure.

track the mouse's movements and the computer responds by moving the cursor on-screen accordingly. Mice are particularly useful with graphics, painting, and design programs.

Printers are the most common peripherals used purely for output, although technically, video displays and modems may also be considered output devices as well. One of the earliest printers was a line printer, developed in 1953 by the Remington Rand Company. Line printers produce entire lines of characters at a time using an engraved band or chain to strike the ribbon.

Printers that produce characters by striking against a ribbon are called impact printers. Another impact printer is the daisy wheel printer, so named for its print mechanism, a spoked wheel containing raised characters. Daisy wheels produce excellent print quality, but print slowly.

Dot matrix printers produce letters in the same fashion as bank temperature signs, whereby light patterns are turned on or off to produce numbers. In the same way, different pin patterns strike the ribbon to produce dot-formed characters. Ink jet printers, a non-impact printer introduced by IBM in 1976, improved upon dot matrix appearance by squirting dots of ink to form letters. In 1982 IBM also introduced the laser printer, an extremely fast printer that utilizes laser beams moving across a rotating drum to create near-typeset-quality print.

Pen plotters, available since the mid-1950s, convert graphs, charts and line drawings into large, high resolution color output. One or several pens move across the paper to produce a 3-D effect image. On the downside, plotters are often bulky (some are as large as pool tables), expensive, and not useful for text output.

With computer output microfilm (COM), developed in 1968, printed output is photographed as very small images on sheets or rolls of film. COM output produces amazing space savings. For instance, a 450-page book can be stored on three 4 x 6 inch (10 x 15 cm) microfiche pages.

See also **Computer disk and tape; Computer network; Computer speech recognition; Computer vision; Digitizer**

⋆⋆ Computer network

Computer networks have helped businesses greatly because they connect different makes and models of **microcomputers**, minicomputers, or even **mainframe computers**, allowing for shared communication, files, and equipment. The first networks appeared in the 1960s when multi-user networks were introduced.

Local area networks, or LANs, which appeared in the early 1970s, are a popular network today. A LAN is a communication network privately owned by the organization using it. The actual distance and number of computers that can be connected is highly dependent upon the type of LAN and communication line used. Telephone lines are sometimes used and are most convenient. However, coaxial cable connections permit faster, higher-quality transmissions. **Fiber optics**, tiny tubes of glass half the diameter of a human hair, has become the preferred technology of the 1990s, allowing faster and less expensive data transmissions than wire cabling.

LANs offer many benefits within companies, industrial sites, college campuses, and hospitals, allowing for more efficient and convenient computer services. Future predictions call for worldwide interconnected networks resembling the telephone systems of today. Accessing these networks will likely become just as commonplace as making a telephone call.

One application of networking, electronic mail (e-mail), introduced in 1984, is very popular among businesses. E-mail service allows letters to be sent across the United States for less than the cost of mail, with the added advantage of arriving within seconds.

Another popular offshoot of networking are information networks, such as CompuServe or the Source, where computer users may access a wide variety of computerized services, including e-mail, investment advice, reference and travel information, shopping, and much more.

See also **Computer input and output devices; Computer operating system**

Future predictions call for worldwide interconnected networks resembling the telephone systems of today. Accessing these networks will likely become just as commonplace as making a telephone call.

⋆⋆⋆ Computer operating system

In early computer systems, a human operator oversaw operations, determined the order of programs to run, and handled all input and output processes. However, much time was wasted when a program would end its run and the entire system sat idle while the operator prepared the next job.

As computer processing speeds increased, the use of human operators became unrealistic. The need for more efficient use of computer resources resulted in the development of operating systems, which act somewhat like traffic directors for the computer.

*The need for
more efficient
use of computer
resources
resulted in the
development of
operating
systems, which
act somewhat
like traffic
directors for
the computer.*

Pioneering Programs

Operating systems are a collection of programs that permit a computer to manage its own operations, including peripherals (printers and modems), programs, and data. In 1954 Gene Amdahl developed the first operating system, which was used on an IBM 704. In 1961 Frederick Brookes, an IBM engineer, began developing an operating system for the IBM S/360. By 1965 Brookes's development team consisted of 2,000 programmers with a budget of $60 million.

Brookes's operating system, known as OS/360, was a well designed, efficient program that became an industry standard for the next several decades. It was the largest software development project ever attempted and remained so through the mid-1980s. OS/360 also served as the basis for other **mainframe computer** software developed in the 1980s, such as DOS/VS, MVS/XA, and OS/VS.

Generally, systems software is developed for a particular type of computer processor chip or to meet a particular function. UNIX, developed in 1971 by Ken Thompson and Denis Ritchie at Bell Laboratories, has become the dominant operating system of the late 1980s and early 1990s. Usable on mainframes, minicomputers, and even **microcomputers**, UNIX is often the preferred operating system for network use. Another mainframe system, PICK, developed by Dick Pick, also goes by the names REALITY, PRIME-INFORMATION, or ULTIMATE, depending upon the type of computer it is used on.

Adapting to Microcomputers

When microcomputers were introduced in the early 1970s, almost all ran under the CP/M operating system, written in 1973 by Gary Kildall. Since its introduction, the CP/M system has been overtaken completely by MS-DOS, an operating system from Microsoft Corporation and its founder William Gates. The earliest version of MS-DOS was based on a product from Seattle Computer Products known as 86-DOS, which was basically an enhanced version of CP/M.

Many powerful features have been added to MS-DOS and current versions bear little resemblance to the first product. Some newer operating systems, including OS/2 introduced in 1987 by Microsoft and IBM, have been hailed as the next industry standard. However, users have been slow to accept a replacement for DOS.

See also **Computer, digital; Computer, industrial uses of; Computer input and output devices; Computer network**

$\overset{\star}{\underset{\star}{\star}}$ Computer simulation

Computer simulation involves designing a model of a real system for the purpose of training, teaching, predicting, or entertaining.

A forerunner of computer simulators was the famous Link trainer used to teach people how to fly in the 1930s. Edwin A. Link, originally a designer of pipe organs and air-powered player pianos, used a device resembling a bellows to twist and turn a cockpit mounted on a movable platform. The "pilot" maneuvered the device by manipulating a mock set of cockpit controls.

Planes and Personalities

More complex flight simulators began using computer graphics starting in 1968. Computer simulation was also used in the field of psychology. Joseph Weizenbaum, who had worked for General Electric and Bank of America in data processing, began a friendship with Kenneth Colby, a psychiatrist who had grown disenchanted with traditional one-to-one psychotherapy (counseling). They believed computers could offer a way of gaining new insights into neurotic (unhealthy) behavior and perhaps even develop new therapeutic methods. Several question-answer machines had been developed already.

The psychoanalytic program ELIZA was such a success that many people spent a great deal of time telling their troubles to the computer.

This led Weizenbaum to try to create a more sophisticated one. The result was ELIZA (named after the character in the musical *My Fair Lady* who learned to speak properly). The program simulated the conversation between a psychoanalyst and a patient, with the machine in the role of the analyst.

The psychoanalytic program was such a success that many people spent a great deal of time telling their troubles to the computer even though they knew it was just a computer program. The key to ELIZA was its natural responses to the statements it received. If it was puzzled by a statement it did not understand, it would fall back on "I see" or "That's very interesting," much as humans do when confused in similar situations.

Approaching Virtual Reality

Probably the most exciting current frontier in the area of computer simulation is virtual reality. This is the most interactive form of simulation. Unlike passive viewing of computer graphics, virtual reality is created by a display and control technology that can surround its user with an artificial environment that attempts to mimic reality.

Important contributors to virtual reality technology include Jaron Lanier, a computer programmer who developed successful video games for Atari in the early 1980s then founded VPL Research, a company that has begun producing a virtual reality headset. Equipped with goggles that contain tiny liquid crystal screens, the headset projects a computer-generated landscape before the user's eyes. Since the image projection program is sensitive to the user's movements, it alters the scene as the user's head moves, producing stunningly realistic images.

Lanier also created a glove called DataGlove with optical fibers and sensors that can measure the position of the wearer's hand and the movement of the fingers. The virtual reality glove allows the wearer to move or grab things in the artificial world presented on the headset. A simplified

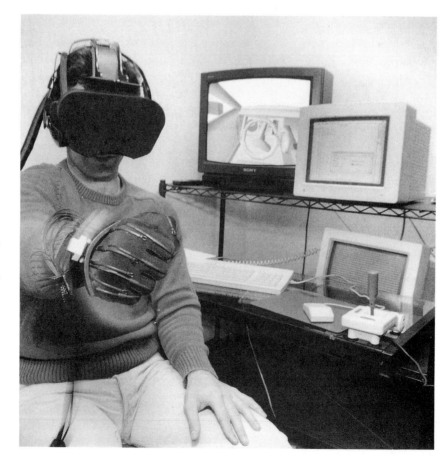

At the offices of VPL Research, one of the pioneers of virtual reality, a staff member wearing an early version of the DataGlove demonstrates a computer that simulates the driving of a car, February 16, 1991.

version of the glove, known as the Power Glove, is sold by Mattel for use with the popular Nintendo video games.

Thomas Furness, a designer of visual displays for the military since 1966, developed a headset in 1982 for use by pilots in the air force similar to the one produced by VPL. He then worked on voice-operated commands that allowed a pilot to look toward a symbol (as the computer tracked the pilot's eye motion), determine what it was, and, if he wanted to shoot at it, utter a word or two to open fire on it.

Finally, Myron Krueger created an artificial reality laboratory at the University of Connecticut in the 1970s, where he has developed virtual reality programs such as CRITTER, a virtual reality cartoon featuring a four-legged yellow creature that interacts with the user.

The tremendous practical potential of computer simulation is just beginning to unfold. Matsushita Corporation of Japan is using virtual reality to help customers shop for custom-built kitchens. The customers can "tour" three-dimensional images of their proposed kitchens using headsets and gloves, suggesting changes before actual installation takes place. Architects and aerospace engineers will be using more simulations in their work as well.

Boeing has already developed a new airliner designed and engineered entirely within a computer. Researchers in drug companies are generating models of molecules to tailor specific drugs for specific conditions. Computer simulation may even become the newest medium for entertainment. VPL Research has formed a joint venture with MCA to build a series of test theaters employing virtual reality on a large scale and forever changing our expectations of entertainment.

The virtual reality glove allows the wearer to move or grab things in the artificial world presented on the headset.

⁎ Computer speech recognition

The invention of machines capable of recognizing human speech has been eagerly anticipated for many years. Prior to 1950, experiments were based upon the idea that language could be analyzed by syntax (the formal structure of a language) and semantics (the meanings of the individual words).

Inventing the Technology

Early speech recognition researchers were convinced that if all the proper word meanings and rules of grammar were stored inside a computer, the machine would be able to effectively translate languages. Unfortunately, more than $20 million was spent by the military and various other government agencies on this type of research—all of which failed miserably.

In the 1950s, the Bell System began experimenting with a system that would allow telephone numbers to be spoken into receivers instead of being dialed, but that project also failed. Many of the problems encountered involved handling variances in accent, pronunciation, background noise, or even speakers with head colds, all of which easily confused the computer.

It began to look as if language translation would never be possible, since interpretation is based to a great extent on understanding, and no one knew what that was, much less how to endow a computer with it. Finally, in 1950 K. H. Davis, an American scientist at Bell Telephone Laboratories, built the first machine able to successfully recognize speech. Davis's machine could distinguish ten spoken numbers from a series of acoustic signals. Industry giants IBM, Nippon Electric Corporation, and Bell Labs have also funded later research projects into voice recognition.

Putting It to Use

Computer speech recognition is used in the education of the handicapped as well as people unable to operate keyboards. A speech recognition system can help hearing-impaired students speak by providing them with a picture when they attempt to form words. Speech recognition has also been used in factories to control machinery, enter data, inspect parts, and take inventory.

In some hospitals, doctors and nurses wear microphones to describe their actions to a computer that interprets and logs instructions and patient records. As more advanced and lower-cost speech recognition chips are being developed, scores of valuable applications and uses for speech recognition systems are being realized.

See also **Computer, digital; Computer, industrial uses of; Computer input and output devices**

As more advanced and lower-cost speech recognition chips are being developed, scores of valuable applications and uses for speech recognition systems are being realized.

⁎ Computer vision

Enabling a computer to "see" is a complex process, involving many factors. In general, images to be analyzed must have any special patterns identified, then precise measurements of the characteristics of the patterns are taken, after which a comparison of each part or pattern takes place. The technology, computer vision (also called machine vision), grew from specialized research into pattern recognition.

Robots That Can See

By the late 1960s, the Massachusetts Institute of Technology (MIT) in Cambridge, Stanford University, and other universities began experimenting with robots capable of seeing. In 1969 the Stanford Institute developed a mobile robot, which they affectionately named "Shakey" for its haphazard way of moving. Outfitted with television cameras coupled to sensory feedback systems, Shakey was an excellent example of early **artificial intelligence** and specialized pattern-recognition technology.

One interesting tangent that arose from computer vision is computer art. An early example produced in 1966 by Bell Lab engineers used a computer linked to a TV camera to scan pictures or paintings. Each row in the picture was separated into points and assigned a number representing brightness. By specifying an appropriate symbol for each number, a fairly accurate rendering of the painting was seen by the computer.

Helping Police and Soldiers

The ability of electronic circuits to "see" an image has also been put to use in Israeli police work. A program called PATREC (short for pattern recognition) has been used to analyze a police artist's sketch of a criminal suspect. Running it through the main police file, similar photographs are matched and selected for further scrutiny.

Computer vision has been used by the military to provide long-distance eyes on the battlefield for military commanders and has proved valuable in analyzing satellite pictures. But perhaps the largest application of machine vision is in the **automobile** manufacturing field. Companies such as General Motors employ thousands of machine vision systems.

Computers have been used to analyze sketches of suspects and then pull matches from police files.

⁎⁎ Concentrated fruit juice

The juice squeezed from raw fruit is marketed today mostly as juice concentrate (juice minus the water content). Even canned and bottled ready-to-drink fruit juice is usually reconstituted (made again) from concentrate.

Gail Borden experimented with producing juice concentrates during the Civil War (1861-65). However, these products were not commercially successful until just after World War II (1939-45), when frozen concentrated orange juice was developed.

A group of citrus growers in Lake Wales, Florida, experimented with alternatives to canned juice, but they did not taste fresh. The growers developed a method of evaporating most of the water from fresh orange juice in an airless tank at temperatures below 80° F. To make up for the loss of some flavor and aroma during evaporation, a small amount of fresh, unconcentrated juice was added back to the concentrate. The resulting mix was then frozen and pasteurized (purified).

Frozen orange juice concentrate was immediately popular with consumers. Even in Florida it far outsells freshly squeezed juice. Other frozen juice concentrates followed, especially apple and grape juices, although they were not nearly as popular as orange juice. Research scientist George Speri Sperti obtained a U.S. patent for freeze-drying orange juice concentrate.

. Contact lens

Contacts are effective when the seeing ability of each eye is different.

Modern contact lenses are thin pieces of **plastic** that fit over the eyeball to correct poor vision. Because they float on a thin film of tears and cover the cornea—the transparent tissue covering the pupil and the iris—they offer the benefits of unimpaired side vision, easy wearability, and near invisibility.

Glass Lenses

The first contact lenses were made by Adolf Fick in 1887. Like eyeglasses, they were made of glass. The first hard-plastic lenses virtually covered the front of the eyeball and were developed in 1938. Although the ability of plastic to correct poor vision was inferior to glass, it proved considerably lighter and more comfortable to wear. Plastic contact lenses were common until the 1950s. The lenses required the doctor to take an impression of the eyeball in order to mold the lenses.

Plastic Lenses

In 1948 Kevin Touhy designed plastic lenses that were smaller than the old lenses and allowed for increased circulation of tears and oxygen.

The development of the keratometer, which takes measurements of the cornea reflected from a light source, eliminated the need for eyeball impressions.

Bifocal contact lenses were first produced in 1958. In 1971 soft or hydrophilic lenses—made from a water-absorbent plastic gel—were developed. Although more comfortable to wear than hard-plastic lenses, soft lenses are easy to damage and must be sterilized before each wearing to avoid any bacterial infection.

Despite their widespread use for cosmetic reasons, contact lenses do offer some medical advantages over eyeglasses. For example, contacts are more effective for restoring sight in people who have had cataracts surgically removed. Contacts are also effective when the seeing ability of each eye is different and are used successfully on people with keratoconus, a condition that causes the cornea to bulge at its center and which cannot be corrected by ordinary glasses.

Contacts can be made in different colors and can be shaded as sunglasses. In addition, they can incorporate magnifying lenses to help people read small print.

✦ Continental drift

Moving Toward an Idea

Early geologists never seriously questioned the stability of Earth's continents until 1620, when the famous philosopher Sir Francis Bacon (1561-1626) pointed out how the Atlantic coastlines of South America and Africa, if pushed together, appeared to be a fit. Likewise, the French naturalist Georges de Buffon suggested in 1750 that North America and Europe had once been joined because of the similarities of their present plants and animals.

For the next 300 years, scientists noticed other similarities between coastlines and fossil remains. They attributed the similarities to narrow land bridges that spanned the distance between the continents, bridges that had since sunk out of sight beneath the surface of the sea.

It was not until the early 1900s when Alfred Lothar Wegener, a German geologist and meteorologist, boldly proposed the explanation for this unusual phenomenon. In his book *The Origin of Continents and*

Two hundred million years ago, all seven continents were joined together in one giant land mass called Pangaea, which floated on a sea of lava.

Oceans, Wegener insisted that 200 million years ago all continents were joined in one land mass called *Pangaea,* or "all-earth," that eventually drifted apart. His theory of continental drift set off a storm of scientific controversy that raged for decades.

Wegener theorized that this large land mass broke into chunks that slowly separated, floating on a basalt (lava) ocean. Over hundreds of millions of years these chunks formed the seven land masses that we now call continents.

Wegener supported his hypothesis with an impressive collection of data. He pointed to the similarities in ancient climatic conditions, matching mountain chains on opposite continents and similar rock types. For instance, the Andes mountains of South America are a continuation of the North American Rockies. And as a result of his intense interest in Greenland, Wegener also came across nineteenth-century records indicating that Greenland moved a mile away from Europe in a century. He also noticed records showing that the North American western coast was moving six feet each year.

Alfred Lothar Wegener insisted that 200 million years ago all continents were joined in one land mass that eventually drifted apart.

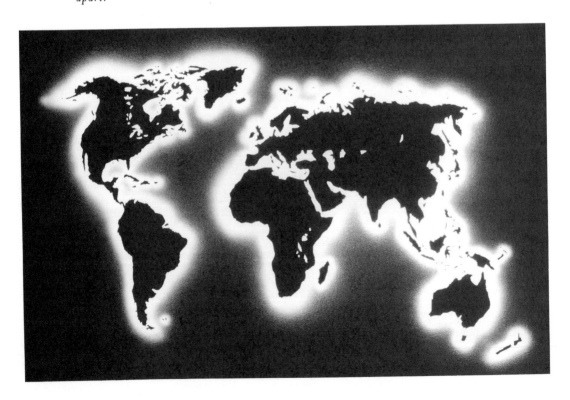

Finding the Cause

Despite the popularity of Wegener's ideas, scientists continued to debate them because he had not formulated a good explanation about what caused the movement. Wegener thought the separation might have been due to the pull of gravitational forces of the Sun and the Moon. But the first explanation was Harry Hammond Hess's, an American geologist who introduced the theory of sea floor spreading in the early 1960s.

*The sea bottom
is continually
expanding and
moving.*

For all the thousands of years that people had been floating, sailing, or steaming across the ocean's surface, the land under water had remained a mystery. In 1945 Hess plumbed the greatest depth of the ocean—about 7 miles (11.3 km). And for the next 20 years, while on the faculty of Princeton University in New Jersey, he continued to study and map the ocean floor.

During this time, Hess discovered the existence of guyots, or peculiar flat-topped protrusions underlying the Pacific Ocean. These isolated submarine mountains, or sea-mounts, rose up from the ocean floor and presented evidence of magma (lava) escaping upwards and creating lava islands, which either sank or eroded away. This fascinating discovery was followed by his finding of oceanic ridges and a massive 10,000-mile-long (16,090 km) submarine mountain chain called the Mid-Atlantic Ridge. This undersea range begins at the southern tip of Africa and snakes its way across the ocean floor to Iceland, averaging 20 miles (32.18 km) in width and rising up to 1 mile (1.609 km) above the ocean floor.

Ocean Floor Movement

By studying the rocks of this massive ridge, geologists learned how the continents probably drifted. Evidence of a deep rift, or trench, running along the crest of the Mid-Atlantic Ridge shows that the sea bottom is continually expanding and moving. This phenomenon is associated with volcanic activity that originates beneath the ocean bottom where molten rock periodically boils out of the ridge. With each underwater volcanic eruption, the deep rift is progressively pulled farther apart.

In 1962 Hess presented evidence demonstrating that the Atlantic seabed was spreading. Some scientists have suggested that the expanding sea bottom is similar to a great conveyor belt: as the ocean bottom spreads, it carries the continents along with it.

Despite the controversy over continental drift just decades ago, most earth scientists now find this theory quite logical in light of the evidence of sea floor spreading. Proof of this phenomenon also supported ideas of the new science of **plate tectonics**, which has built upon the continental drift theory and is itself central to the new geology. Both theories suggest that the map of 1995 might look significantly different in another million years or so.

⋆⁺⋆ Cortisone

Cortisone is one of several steroid **hormones** secreted by the human body. Some hormones control sugar **metabolism** (digestion), while others control the metabolism of minerals and water. Cortisone's job is to quickly convert protein to the carbohydrate glucose and regulate salt metabolism. Cortisone also helps the body withstand stress. It is used medically to reduce inflammation (swelling).

Cortisone's first successful medical use was for treatment of rheumatoid arthritis. However, treatments were discontinued when researchers found that rheumatoid arthritis is not caused by hormone deficiency.

Cortisone treatments have some serious side effects. These include edema (fluid build up), high stomach acidity, and abnormal metabolism of **sodium**, **potassium**, and **nitrogen**. Further experiments, however, yielded a refined product that reduced the side effects.

Today cortisone is prescribed to reduce inflammation in **allergy** cases and in arthritis and other connective tissue diseases. It is also prescribed as a replacement hormone in Addison's disease (loss of strength), and for people whose adrenal glands (near the kidneys) have been removed. Other uses include cancer therapy and reduction of the body's immune response to prevent rejection of transplanted organs.

⋆⁺⋆ Cosmetics

Archaeological evidence found at cavemen's sites indicates that prehistoric peoples used various pigments (colors) mixed with grease to paint not only the walls of their caves but also their bodies. Body painting, in addition to being considered ornamental, was thought to give supernatural protection. At some burial sites, large quantities of paints have been found with the dead. Archaeologists have identified 17 different colors in use in prehistoric times. The most popular were white, black, orange, red, and yellow.

Ancient Egypt and the Roman Empire

Both historical records and archaeological evidence show that the

Ancient Egyptian queen Nefertiti wore an eyeliner made from ground ants' eggs and kohl, a paste made from soot, antimony, or galena.

ancient peoples of the Middle East also used cosmetics for decorative as well as religious purposes. Their lavish use of eye cosmetics seems to have served the additional purpose of warding off the glare of the sun. Eye cosmetics included an eyeliner made from ground ants' eggs and kohl, a paste made from soot, antimony, or galena (a type of lead ore) that was applied to the eyelashes, lids, and brows. Two famous Egyptian queens who adorned themselves in this manner were Nefertiti (c. 1365 B.C.) and, much later, Cleopatra (c. 50 B.C.).

Also in common use among the upper classes of Egypt were rouges, henna (a reddish color) for dying hair and fingernails, white powders, bath oils, and abrasives for cleaning teeth. The oldest cosmetic item that archaeologists have found in the Middle East is one in common use today—lipstick. It was found in a Babylonian tomb dating from about 4000 B.C., and in all likelihood belonged to a man.

Although the word "cosmetics" derives from the Greek *kosmetikos,* meaning "skilled in decorating," the classical Greeks apparently frowned on the use of cosmetics. Similarly, the early Romans regarded cosmetics as a sign of bad character. With the rise of the Roman Empire, however, and the luxurious goods imported from the conquered lands of the Middle East, cosmetics became status symbols for Romans of both sexes.

The Crusaders Visit the Middle East

Throughout Europe, Roman attention to personal cleanliness and beauty died as the Empire went into decline. These customs did not reemerge until the Crusaders began returning from the Holy Land (Israel) in the Middle Ages A.D. (400-1450). The medieval ideal of Caucasian feminine beauty—skin white as a lily and cheeks of rosy red—was pursued by nobility and commoners alike. But while the ruling class could afford expensive cosmetics, their subjects had to whiten their skin with wheat flour and rouge their cheeks with beet juice.

By the 1500s, the French had become famous for their skill in applying cosmetics. High-born men and women powdered their hair with saffron (a flower) or flower pollen and painted their faces with "supernatural luster," a preparation of gold leaf and hot lemon juice. Venice (Italy), however, was the major producer of cosmetics. A skin whitener known as Venetian ceruse was very popular, even though it was known that the white lead it contained could damage the skin and result in baldness or even death. Other dangerous concoctions included red mercuric sulfide, used for lipstick, and sulfuric acid, used for bleaching hair.

While the medieval ruling class could afford expensive cosmetics, their subjects had to whiten their skin with wheat flour and rouge their cheeks with beet juice.

The French Court

Cosmetics had their heyday in eighteenth-century Europe, where the ideal of beauty seems to have been a completely unreal appearance. Members of the French court whitened their faces and etched the veins of their faces in blue. Beauty patches of black silk or velvet, originally invented as small dots or crescents to hide the disfiguring marks of smallpox, became larger and took the form of flowers, stars, birds, and symbols of personal occupation and politics.

With the French Revolution and the dawn of the Victorian Age, cosmetics again went into decline. Men would not wear them, and respectable women adhered to the Victorian ideal of a "natural" beauty, where anything more than a dab of rice powder or scent was considered improper.

Impact of Advertising and Movies

But by the late 1800s, advertising was coming into its own, including endorsements such as that of Pear's Soap by the English actress Lillie Langtry. Once again respectable women began experimenting with cosmetics. It was not until the 1920s, however, when **motion pictures** and movie stars were becoming the rage, that cosmetics started growing into

The oldest cosmetic item that archaeologists have found in the Middle East is one in common use today—lipstick. More than $1 billion is spent on lipstick a year.

the multimillion-dollar industry that it is today. Two entrepreneurs who contributed significantly to the rise of the cosmetics trade were Elizabeth Arden (1884-1966) and Helena Rubinstein (1870-1965), whose rivalry became well known to Americans.

Born in Poland, Helena Rubinstein immigrated to Australia in 1902 with a fair complexion and 12 pots of her mother's face cream, the invention of a European chemist. Australian women were so impressed with Rubinstein's skin that she was finally persuaded to open a small beauty shop in Melbourne.

By 1908 Rubinstein had fashionable salons in London and Paris. In 1915, with World War I (1914-18) underway, she fled to the United States, where she proceeded to open salons in New York, Boston, Philadelphia, and San Francisco. In the "flapper" era that followed the war, she created the vamp look for the movie actress Theda Bara (1890-1955). Madame, as Rubinstein was known, died in 1965 at the age of 94, leaving an estate valued at more than $130 million.

Elizabeth Arden's career was as meteoric as that of Rubinstein. Born into a family of British immigrants in rural Ontario, Canada, Arden became one of the wealthiest women in the world. At one time, she operated more than 100 salons on three continents.

Although early in her career she tutored herself by having a facial at almost every salon in Paris, even at that stage she would not deign to visit the salon of her arch-rival, Rubinstein. In 1938, in one memorable episode, Arden hired away a dozen members of Rubinstein's New York salon. Not to be outdone, Madame retaliated by hiring Arden's former husband and business partner.

Despite—or perhaps helped by—such well-publicized skirmishes, the modern cosmetics industry grew. Aided by improvements in **mass production**, packaging, and advertising techniques and safety regulated in the United States since 1938 by federal legislation, cosmetics is today one of the world's major industries.

See also **Hair care; Toothbrush and toothpaste**

⁎ Cretaceous catastrophe

Mass extinctions of many animal species have occurred throughout geologic history. But one of the world's great mysteries is the unexplainable disappearance of the great dinosaurs at the end of the Cretaceous period, approximately 65 million years ago. Some scientists think severe changes in the Earth's environment is the cause, while others think shrinking seas and widespread disease killed the dinosaurs. Still others believe the dinosaurs' death might have been the result of a huge disaster such as a meteor hit, but conclusive evidence has not been found.

Support for Outer Space Theory

In 1980 a team of scientists headed by Walter Alvarez (1940-) proposed the Cretaceous catastrophe theory. This theory asserts that an enormous catastrophe marked the end of the Cretaceous period, causing the extinction of the dinosaurs. Alvarez, his father, Luis W. Alvarez (1911-1988), who received the 1968 Nobel Prize in physics, and scientists Frank Asaro and Helen Michel published their findings in the June 6, 1980, issue of *Science* magazine.

In their study, the team demonstrated that Earth had been hit by an asteroid roughly the size of Manhattan. First they discovered high levels of the metal iridium layered between Cretaceous and Tertiary rock formations in Denmark, Italy, and New Zealand. Next they theorized that a great extraterrestrial (space) object or objects crashed into Earth. The impact not

In 1980 a team of scientists headed by Walter Alvarez proposed that during the Cretaceous period Earth was hit by a great asteroid, consequently causing the extinction of the dinosaurs. Evidence of a massive crash was discovered in the Yucatán region of Mexico in 1992.

PRECAMBRIAN

PALEOZOIC	CAMBRIAN
	ORDOVICIAN
	SILURIAN
	DEVONIAN
	MISSISSIPPIAN
	PENNSYLVANIAN
	PERMIAN
MESOZOIC	TRIASSIC
	JURASSIC
	CRETACEOUS
CENOZOIC	TERTIARY
	QUATERNARY

UNITED STATES

MEXICO

Gulf of Mexico

Yucatan Peninsula

only left a sizable dent, it probably sent a blanket of dust into the atmosphere, blocking sunlight and gradually disrupting plant life and other ecosystems everywhere.

Their theory, backed as it was by geologic evidence, drew initial support in the scientific community, but it still lacked the final key to solving the mystery: If such a massive meteor had such a powerful impact, why were its remains still undiscovered? Part of the problem lies in the geologic processes of Earth. Since the time of the crash, approximately 20 percent of Earth's crust has been absorbed into the interior of the surface through a process called subduction. This means that geologists have to dig deeper into layers of rock and dirt to find current evidence.

Meteor Site Is Found

The purported crater remained missing until the early 1990s, when several scientific teams began to uncover evidence in the Gulf of Mexico

Centered near the town of Chicxulub on the north coast, the crater extends into the Gulf of Mexico and measures 112 miles (180 km) in diameter.

Satellite image of the impact crater on the Yucatán peninsula. Rocks found in this area are comprised of quartz grains showing the shock waves of an impact.

region. Then, in 1992, another team led by Alan Hildebrand of the Geological Survey of Canada in Ottawa announced the discovery of a large crater in the Yucatán region of Mexico that left ample evidence of a massive crash.

Rocks found in this area were comprised of quartz grains showing the shock waves of an impact. This provided the much-needed evidence to back up earlier discoveries. Actually, the Mexican national petroleum company (PEMEX) had begun uncovering clues as early as the 1950s. While drilling exploratory wells in the Yucatán region, they penetrated layers of rocks, unusual for that region. Upon careful study, geologists discovered that these rocks had solidified from a molten state.

In the 1970s, PEMEX conducted a magnetic survey of the area, which revealed a large circular structure buried beneath the surface. Centered near the town of Chicxulub on the north coast, the circle extended into the Gulf of Mexico and measured 112 miles (180 km) in diameter. Despite the magnitude of these discoveries, PEMEX had not released the information.

One more puzzle piece clicks into place with the asteroid theory. Why weren't mammals wiped out when the dinosaurs were? Because being smaller they could survive on much less food, could adapt more easily to changes in the environment, and probably survived on dinosaur carcasses and rotting vegetation.

⁎⋆ Cruise control, automobile

Ralph Teeter was blinded in an accident at the age of eight, but this tragedy did not prevent him from building his own **gasoline**-powered car at the age of twelve and later going on to earn an engineering degree from the University of Pennsylvania in Philadelphia.

On a trip to visit the university in the 1930s, Teeter realized during the drive that few motorists maintained a constant speed on the long stretches of the Pennsylvania Turnpike. Relying on the sound of their **automobile**'s engines and the feel of the vibrations, he sensed that drivers were moving at uneven and inconsistent speeds, a problem that could lead to accidents and wasted gasoline.

Near the end of World War II (1939-45), Teeter completed his system of cruise control, called a Speedostat. His device essentially allowed the driver to select a speed by dialing a number. When the car reached that

Cruise control kept gas use steady and helped increase drivers' awareness of road conditions.

speed, the accelerator would resist further pressure. The driver did have the ability to increase the speed by exerting extra pressure on the gas pedal. This early mechanism only prevented drivers from moving at speeds higher than those they had selected. It did not allow them to maintain a steady speed.

To create the first true cruise control, Teeter added a magnet to his invention. This allowed a simple lock-in device to function, permitting the driver to maintain the same speed without pressing the accelerator, regardless of the terrain or wind resistance. This version of cruise control soon replaced the Speedostat.

Cruise control was not an immediate success, since motorists were often unsure of its benefits. Some felt that relying on cruise control was not safe since it might increase the boredom of the ride and lead to less driver awareness. Others, however, acknowledged the control's advantages to the driver, who was free to devote greater attention to the road.

By 1956 cruise control systems were manufactured by a larger company that improved the design and marketed the product more aggressively. Today, 70 percent of all new American cars are equipped with cruise control. Teeter himself went on to invent more than 20 other products and was granted some 50 U.S. patents.

⋆⋆⋆ Cryogenics

The science of cryogenics is closely related to the commercial process of refrigeration.

The term "cryogenics" comes from the Greek word *kruos,* for "frost." The science of cryogenics is closely related to the commercial process of refrigeration, and progress in one field is often the result of progress in the other.

The origin of cryogenic research is often associated with the first liquefaction of **oxygen**, **nitrogen**, and **carbon monoxide** gas. This discovery allowed people to attain low temperatures by compressing one of these gases as much as possible.

An important development in early cryogenics research was the development of an efficient system for storing liquefied gases. That system was invented by the Scottish chemist James Dewar in 1891. The Dewar flask is well known today as the vacuum flask used to keep liquids hot or cold. The flask consists of a double-walled bottle containing a vacuum between the two silvered walls. The vacuum prevents loss or entry of heat by conduction or convection, and the silvering causes heat to reflect inward into or outward out of the container.

By the early 1900s, every gas had yielded to liquefaction except **hydrogen** and **helium**. Then, between 1906 and 1908, the Dutch physicist Heike Kamerlingh Onnes achieved success, first with hydrogen, then with helium.

Further cryogenic research demanded the development of new cooling techniques. In the mid-1920s, the method of adiabatic demagnetization was proposed independently by Peter Debye and W. F. Giauque. In this process, the material to be cooled is placed in contact with a paramagnetic field and with liquid helium and then subjected to a strong **magnetic field**.

Perhaps best known and commercially most significant of all low-temperature phenomena is **superconductivity,** the tendency of a material to lose all electrical resistance at low temperatures. Originally observed at temperatures no greater than a few degrees Kelvin, superconductivity has now been reported at temperatures as high as 100° K.

A number of commercial applications of cryogenics have been suggested. Freezing with liquid nitrogen is now a standard method of food preservation. A similar technique has been proposed for preserving humans with incurable diseases, with the view to thawing them at some time in the future when a cure for the disease has been found. One of the important uses of superconductivity in research is in the construction of magnets used in very large **particle accelerators,** which are used, among other things, for the study of atoms.

$\star_\star^\star$ Curium

Elements 95 and 96 were both discovered in 1944 during war-related (World War II, 1939-45) research in the Metallurgical Research Laboratory at the University of Chicago.

By 1947 a visible quantity of the first pure compound of element 96 had been prepared. The element had, by that time, been given the name "curium," in honor of Marie and Pierre Curie, codiscoverers of radium. Some scientists believe that a form of curium was present at the creation of Earth and was a parent of the lower members of the actinide (radioactive) family of elements. Even with a half life of 16 million years, all remaining quantities of the original sample have long since decayed.

The first sample of pure metallic curium was produced in 1951. The metal is hard, silvery, and brittle, with a melting point of 2444° F (1340° C).

Curium generates an unusually large amount of energy as it decays. This property has made it useful in small, compact power sources at remote locations on Earth and in space vehicles. The element is also highly toxic (poisonous).

⁎ Cybernetics

A robot welder at the General Motors plant in Lordstown, Ohio, 1983. By the 1960s and 1970s, a large number of industrial and manufacturing plants devised and installed cybernetic systems such as robots in the workplace.

Cybernetics is the study of communication and feedback control in machines and humans. Cybernetics analyzes the ability of humans, animals, and some machines to respond to or make adjustments based upon input from the environment. This process of response or adjustment is called "feedback" or "automatic control."

For example, the household thermostat uses feedback when it turns a furnace on or off based on its measurements of temperature. The earliest known feedback control mechanism, the centrifugal governor, was developed by Scotsman James Watt in 1788. Watt's steam engine governor kept the engine at a constant rate.

Systems for Guiding Missiles

The principles of feedback control were first clearly defined by Norbert Wiener (1894-1964), a American mathematician. With his colleague, Julian Bigelow, Wiener worked for the U.S. government during World War II (1939-45), developing **radar** and missile guidance systems using automatic information processing and machine controls.

After the war Wiener continued to work in machine and human feedback research. The word "cybernetics," coined by Wiener, comes from a Greek word *kybernetes,* meaning "steersman." In *The Human Use of Human Beings: Cybernetics and Society,* published in 1950, Wiener cautioned that an increased reliance on machines might start a decline in human intellectual capabilities.

Cybernetics and Industry

With the advent of the **digital computer**, cybernetic principles such as those described by Wiener could be applied to increasingly complex tasks. The result was machines with the practical ability to carry out meaningful work. In 1946 Delmar S. Harder devised one of the earliest such systems to automate the manufacture of car engines at the Ford Motor Company. The system involved an element of thinking—the machines regulated themselves, without human supervision, to produce the desired results. Harder's assembly-line automation produced one car engine every 14 minutes—compared with the 21 hours it had previously taken humans.

By the 1960s and 1970s, the fields of cybernetics, **robotics**, and **artificial intelligence** began to skyrocket. A large number of industrial and manufacturing plants devised and installed cybernetic systems such as robots in the workplace. In 1980 there were roughly about 5,000 industrial robots in the United States. By the year 2000, researchers estimate there could be half a million.

See also **Computer, digital; Computer, industrial uses of; Computer operating system; Mass production**

✦ Cystic fibrosis

Cystic fibrosis is an inherited (genetic) disease that affects about 1 out of every 2,000 Caucasians of European descent, and it is the leading fatal genetic disease in the United States. The disease is less common in African Americans and very rare in Asians and Native Americans.

Cystic fibrosis is characterized by a thick mucus that accumulates in the lungs, pancreas, and intestine. It can be fatal if the mucus blocks the lungs. Patients may suffer from **pneumonia** caused by bacterial infections. Other serious complications include respiratory (breathing) failure, diabetes, enlarged heart, liver cirrhosis, intestinal blockage, pancreatic dysfunction, **sodium** (salt) deficiency, and sterility (inability to have children).

Abdominal (stomach) cramps, malnutrition, growth retardation, and coughing are all symptoms associated with cystic fibrosis. However, the increased saltiness of sweat is the most useful test to diagnose the disease. It is difficult to predict when any of these symptoms will appear or how severe they will be. While the disease used to be fatal to nearly all children who developed it, more than 50 percent of cystic fibrosis patients now live longer than 20 years.

While there are treatments available for cystic fibrosis, there is no cure. Often, antihistamine and decongestants are prescribed to open air passages. Cough suppressants are avoided since coughing helps to loosen the mucus in the trachea and lungs. **Antibiotics** help to treat pneumonia. Physical therapy and surgery have also been used.

✲ Dacron

"Dacron" is one of the names the Du Pont company uses for a **polymer** fiber—**polyethylene** terephthalate—that John Whinfield and J. T. Dickinson developed in Great Britain in 1941. Whinfield and Dickinson called their new **synthetic fiber** Terylene.

Dacron revolutionized the textile industry.

Nylon, invented by Wallace Hume Carothers, an American chemist at Du Pont, had been doing a booming business since its introduction in 1935. Rayon, invented in 1892, was another synthetic fiber in high demand. At the time Whinfield and Dickinson were working on Terylene, the race to develop substitutes for natural fibers was on. World War II (1939-45) was being fought and many sources of natural cloths such as cotton and silk were closed. Any similar product stood a good chance of being successful and contributing to the war effort.

Making Cloth From Chemicals

Despite intensive research at Du Pont, Carothers had found the fibers of most **polyesters** unsuitable for use in textiles (cloth and rugs) because of their low melting temperatures. The one reaction Carothers and his team had not tried was the one Whinfield and Dickinson used to create polyethylene terephthalate.

Dacron fibers are made by heating the polymer and forcing it through a metal plate with small holes. The fibers are drawn out and passed through a pair of rollers rotating at different speeds. Through a series of steps, the strands are strengthened and interwoven. Dacron also offers a high melting temperature of 496° F (256° C).

The discovery of Dacron revolutionized the textile industry, since it was one of the first artificial fibers and was used both in wool blends and by itself. Hundreds of tons of Dacron are produced each year.

See also **Fiber, synthetic; Polymer and polymerization**

⋆⋆ DDT
(dichloro-diphenyl-trichloroethane)

DDT (dichloro-diphenyl-trichloroethane) is a synthetic (manufactured) insecticide. This colorless, odorless liquid kills a variety of insects such as flies, lice, mosquitoes, and agricultural pests.

When applied to an insect, DDT is easily absorbed through the body surface, and after attacking the nervous system, causes paralysis. Some insects, however, have developed a resistance to DDT, which makes the insecticide ineffective. These resistant insects are able to reproduce and pass this trait on to their offspring. This immune process has taken many years to develop.

The benefits of DDT were demonstrated in the 1940s. In World War II (1939-45), the insecticide was used to clear out mosquito-infested areas before troops were sent in. Even after the war, the use of DDT in the United States almost completely wiped out malaria and yellow fever. And in tropical areas, the use of DDT has helped save millions of lives that would otherwise have been lost to disease. For years DDT was routinely applied as a crop dust or water spray on orchards, gardens, fields, and forests. At one point it was registered for use on 334 agricultural crops.

DDT is extremely durable. In some applications, it continues to kill bugs for 12 years. Water cannot wash it away and it resists breakdown by light and air. This strength and persistence has resulted in some problems with DDT. For instance, the solution of DDT can transfer to non-target living organisms. Once in an ecosystem, it can pass on from crops to birds and from water to fish, eventually affecting the whole food chain.

*Opposite page:
Spraying oranges
for aphids and red
spiders in Southern
California.*

When eaten by humans, DDT is stored in body fats and can be passed on to nursing babies. Low levels of DDT in humans are harmless but large concentrations can cause severe health problems such as liver cancer.

Eureka!

By the 1950s, it became clear that DDT harmed the environment and human health. Rachel Carson's landmark study, *Silent Spring* (1962), exposed the dangers of unregulated pesticide use. Spurred by public pressure, state and federal governments turned their attention to the regulation of pesticides. In 1972 the U.S. Environmental Protection Agency banned the use of DDT. Today, DDT is restricted in the United States, Europe, and Japan. However, many other countries still use DDT widely for malaria control, delousing, and the killing of other disease-spreading insects.

Through her 1962 book Silent Spring, *Rachel Carson exposed the dangers of unregulated pesticide use.*

✦ Decimal system

Historians believe that our decimal system originated with the ancient practice of counting on fingers, first with one hand, later with both hands. With 10 fingers as a starting point, the number 10 was a natural for our number base. In fact, the word "decimal" is derived from the Latin word for 10. Base 60 was the earliest numbering system among the ancient Mesopotamian civilizations in the Middle East (beginning with the Sumerians). Remnants of the base 60 system are still evident today in our division of degrees, hours, and minutes.

Other Cultures Use Base 10

By 300 B.C., India had adopted and modified the Middle Eastern system, changing from base 60 to base 10. However, the base 10 system was also evident in China around the same period, and history often credits both civilizations with developing the decimal system. A plate of East Indian origin, containing the date A.D. 346 in decimal form, is the oldest evidence of Indian use.

We use a base 10 system today because our ancestors learned to count by using their fingers.

In the early sixth century the Indian astronomer Arybhata produced an important book, also called *Arybhata*. The book contained astronomical tables, a study of arithmetic, time and measure, and the sphere of Earth. The arithmetic section included counting by 10 up to 10 to the eighth power (or 10^8) and written procedures for using a system of nine numerals and a tenth sign that functioned as a zero.

From China and India, the decimal system may have spread to Persia (Iran) and Egypt, and later it became widely used in Arabia and Greece. With the introduction of Hindu-Arabic numerals into Europe in the twelfth century, the system evolved into the familiar decimal system used almost universally today.

Scottish mathematician John Napier (best known for his invention of **logarithms** in 1614) also developed his own base two (**binary**) system. Today's computers operate on a form of the binary system using "on" and "off" electric pulses. Napier also was the first to make popular the decimal point to separate a whole number from the fractional part of a number.

⋆⋆ Decompression sickness

Many people often feel pressure when flying in airplanes. Their ears seem to "pop" and their balance is affected. Like fliers, deep sea and scuba divers experience the drastic change in **atmospheric pressure** as they descend into the water and return to the surface. Airplanes are pressurized, however, and the passengers usually experience only mild changes in air pressure, unlike divers who must experience it firsthand.

Ascending (rising) too rapidly from deep waters can result in decompression sickness, also called the bends, and compressed air illness. In the very worst cases, people can become paralyzed and die from decompression sickness. Milder symptoms are pain in the joints and muscles. This pain can occur after the diver has reached deep waters and the pressure increase has had an impact on both the diver's body and the air he or she breathes.

If the diver stays deep beneath the surface for a long time, gases, especially **nitrogen**, will accumulate in his or her body tissues. If the diver surfaces too quickly, these nitrogen gases expand and form bubbles in various parts of the body. When the bubbles develop in nerves or muscles, they can cause pain. When they occur in the spinal cord or brain, the diver can become dizzy, blind, and even paralyzed. If the bubbles form in the lungs, the diver can choke, first experiencing rapid shallow breathing and ultimately death.

Diving has become a much safer sport, since divers now use stage decompression, in which the diver stops every couple of feet while rising

A plaque at the entrance to Old Port Royal in Jamaica, West Indies, remembers an early diver who died of "the bends" at age 25 in 1862.

to the surface. If the diver waits for a couple of minutes at each level, the gases in the body tissues are allowed to adjust to the new pressure.

Today, this approach has been modernized through the use of the decompression chamber. The diver is placed at the surface in a large sealed container which simulates the stages of decompression.

⁎⁎ Dental drill

George Washington's dentist invented the first known "dental foot engine" in 1790 by adapting his mother's foot-treadle spinning wheel to rotate a drill.

When a tooth develops a cavity, the decayed part must be removed. The earliest devices for doing this were picks and enamel scissors. Then two-edged cutting instruments were designed; they were twirled in both directions between the fingers. The father of modern dentistry, the Frenchman Pierre Fauchard (1678-1761), described an improved drill in 1728. Its rotating movement was powered by catgut twisted around a cylinder, or by jewelers' bowstrings. A hand-cranked dental drill bit was patented by John Lewis in 1838.

Dentistry Enters the Modern Age

The Scottish inventor James Nasmyth used a coiled wire spring to drive a drill in 1829. Charles Merry of St. Louis, Missouri, adapted Nasmyth's drill, adding a flexible cable, in 1858.

The first "motor-driven" drill appeared in 1864 and was the design of Englishman George F. Harrington. This handheld drill was powered by the spring action of a **clock** movement. In 1868 the American George F. Green introduced a pneumatic drill powered by a pedal bellows.

Fellow American James B. Morrison patented a pedal bur drill in 1871. A further improvement of the Nasmyth-Merry design, it featured a flexible arm with a "hand" piece to hold the drill, plus a foot treadle and pulleys. Each of these advances increased the speed at which the drill operated.

In 1874 Green added electricity to the dental drill. It worked well but was heavy and expensive. Plug-in electric drills became available in 1908 because by then most dental offices were electrified. Once efficient, mechanically driven drills became widely available, teeth could be properly and accurately prepared for well-fitting crowns and fillings. American teeth blossomed with gold.

Modern dental drills are turbine-powered and rotate at speeds of 300,000 to 400,000 revolutions per minute.

See also **Dental filling, crown, and bridge**

⁎⋆ Dental filling, crown, and bridge

Fillings

Cavities in teeth have been filled since earliest times with a variety of materials including stone chips, turpentine resin, gum, and metals. Arculanus (Giovanni d'Arcoli) recommended gold-leaf fillings in 1484. The renowned physician Ambroise Paré (1510-1590) used lead or cork to fill teeth. In the 1700s, Pierre Fauchard (1678-1761), the father of modern dentistry, favored tin foil or lead cylinders. Philip Pfaff (1715-1767), dentist to Frederick the Great of Prussia (1712-1786), used gold foil to cap the pulp. But the invention of the power-driven **dental drill** led to increased demand for fillings and also for an inexpensive filling material.

Auguste Taveau of Paris, France, developed what was probably the first dental amalgam—a solution of one or more metals in mercury—in 1826. He used filings from silver coins mixed with mercury. When the French Crawcour brothers immigrated to the United States in 1833, they introduced Taveau's amalgam. The poor quality of the amalgam led to its condemnation by many dentists, kicking off the so-called "amalgam war," a ten-year period from 1840 to 1850 of bitter controversy about the merits of mercury amalgam. The Chicago dentist G. V. Black (1836-1915) finally standardized both cavity preparation and amalgam manufacture in 1895.

After truly effective dental cement was developed, baked porcelain inlays came into use for filling large cavities. In 1897 an Iowa dentist, B. F. Philbrook, described his method of casting metallic fillings from a wax impression that matched the shape of the cavity perfectly. William H. Taggart of Chicago described a similar method for casting gold inlays in 1907. This technique made possible the modern era of accurate filling and inlay fitting.

Made of gold and used by the Etruscans 2,500 years ago, crowns and bridges fell out of use during the Middle Ages and were only gradually rediscovered.

Crowns and Bridges

Crowns are used to replace and cover missing portions of teeth. Bridges are mountings for artificial teeth attached at either end to natural teeth. Made of gold and used by the Etruscans 2,500 years ago, crowns and bridges fell out of use during the Middle Ages (A.D. 400-1450) and were only gradually rediscovered.

Bridge work developed as crowns did. Dentists would add extra facing to a crown to hold a replacement for an adjacent missing tooth. The major advance came with the detachable facings patented by Walter Mason of New Jersey in 1890 and the improved interchangeable facings introduced by Mason's associate Thomas Steele in 1904. The common problem of broken facings was now easy to fix, and permanent bridge installation became possible and successful.

⋆⋆ Desalination techniques

Approximately 97 percent of the water on Earth is undrinkable by humans.

Desalination is the process of removing salt from sea water. The process, also known as desalinization, desalting, or saline water reclamation, has been studied for thousands of years, which is not surprising given the human need for water and the lack of fresh water in many areas. Approximately 97 percent of the water on Earth is either sea water or brackish (salt water contained in inland bodies), such as the Great Salt Lake of Utah. Both are undrinkable by humans.

The method used to decrease the salt level depends on the local water supply, the water needs of the community, and economics. Other considerations are growing populations in arid (dry) or desert lands, contaminated groundwater, and sailors at sea who need fresh water to drink.

Early Attempts to Desalt Water

In the fourth century B.C., philosopher Aristotle (384-322 B.C.) told of Greek sailors desalting water by using evaporation. Another technique used a wool wick to siphon the water. The salts were trapped in the wool. During the first century A.D. the Romans employed clay filters to trap salt. Distillation was widely used from the fourth century on—salt water was boiled and the steam collected in sponges. The first scientific paper on desalting was published by Arab chemists in the eighth century. The techniques have become more sophisticated, but distillation and filtering are still the primary methods of desalination for most of the world.

Modern Methods

The first desalination patent was granted in 1869 and in that same year the first land-based steam distillation plant was established in Britain, to replenish the fresh water supplies of the ships at anchor in the harbor.

A constant problem in such a process is scaling. When the water is heated over 160° F (71° C), the dissolved solids in water will appear as a crusty residue known as scale. The scale interferes with the desalting machinery, greatly reducing the effectiveness.

Distillation and filtering are still the primary methods of desalination for most of the world.

The majority of desalting plants today use a procedure known as multistage flash distillation to avoid scale. Lowering the pressure on the sea water allows it to boil at temperatures below 160° F, avoiding scaling. The water is boiled many times. The entire process takes advantage of thermodynamic laws to get the maximum use of any energy. It is the reuse of heat that makes these plants economical. Over 80 percent of land-based desalting plants are multistage flash distillation facilities.

A host of other desalination processes have been developed. An increasingly popular process, reverse osmosis, essentially filters water at the molecular level by forcing it through a membrane. Membranes have been steadily improving with the introduction of **polymers** (**plastics**).

Solar distillation is used in the subtropical regions of the world. Sea water is placed in a black tray and covered by a sloping sheet of glass or plastic. Sunlight passes through the cover. Water evaporates and then condenses on the cover. It runs down the cover and is collected. The salts are left behind in the trays. This method has been used successfully in the Greek islands.

See also **Polymer and polymerization**

⋆⋆ Dialysis machine

The kidneys are vital to human health because they filter waste materials out of the blood. When the kidneys stop functioning, a person dies quickly from waste buildup.

As early as 1861 a Scottish chemist, Thomas Graham (1748-1843), described a procedure he called dialysis to purify the **blood** in cases of kidney failure. Graham proposed that the blood be diffused across a membrane that allowed wastes to drop out.

For dialysis to work, a major problem had to be overcome. The blood tended to clot or form lumps while circulating in the tubes of early dialysis machines. The addition of an anticoagulant (a solution that stopped clotting) solved this problem.

Dialysis has saved many lives by performing the cleansing functions of kidneys.

Dialysis has made possible the transplanting of kidneys—the first organs to be successfully transplanted. The dialysis machine keeps patients alive until their new kidney starts to function. The machines also maintain patients whose kidneys have failed until a donated organ becomes available.

Long-term dialysis treatment became possible in 1960 when Belding Scribner of Seattle designed a Teflon and Silastic shunt (two parallel tubes with a U-connection) that could be inserted into a patient's artery and vein and left in place for months or years. The fistula, an internal surgical connection of an artery with a vein, was developed in 1966. Home dialysis was pioneered by doctors in Boston and London beginning in 1964.

⋆⋆ Diaper, disposable

Luvs were designed by Kenneth Buell, who had worked on the Gemini space project.

Before the wide-spread use of the disposable diaper in the 1960s, babies wore soggy cloth nappies, which their parents washed, bleached, and dried. Tired of diapers that had to be washed or sent to an expensive laundry service, New York homemaker Marion Donovan used some absorbent padding and a piece of shower curtain to invent the first disposable diaper, called the Boater, in 1951.

Manufacturers were skeptical of the snap-on, throwaway diaper, so Donovan marketed her product herself. Her diaper grew more and more popular and Donovan eventually sold her interest in the product for $1 million.

The first mass-produced disposable diapers were not very comfortable or leakproof. However, by the late 1950s, Procter and Gamble (P&G) had begun research and development of the disposable diaper. It is said that P&G spent more research money on diapers than Henry Ford spent on the first automobile.

The company's first effort was a pair of **plastic** pants with elasticized waistband and leg openings, but this product never gained much popularity. In 1961 Procter and Gamble introduced Pampers, the rayon-plastic-fluff model that would set the standard and lead the market for diapers for the next several decades. By 1975 the company unveiled another brand called Luvs (designed by Kenneth Buell, also known for his work on the Gemini space program).

Improvements to the basic disposable diaper design have included adhesive tabs to replace the awkward and potentially dangerous diaper pin and separate models specially designed for boy and girl babies.

By the 1980s, studies showed that most babies wore disposable diapers. Although disposable diaper manufacturers and their fans claim that disposable diapers make up only tiny percentages of landfill waste, some families concerned about the environmental implications of disposable diapers are returning to cloth diapers.

See also **Polymer and polymerization**

⁎⋆ **Digestion**

All living creatures need some type of food to keep their bodies healthy and to give them the energy they need to get their work done. Digestion is

The ancient Greeks believed food was digested by body heat. The scientists of the 1600s thought the process was fermentation.

A Window Into the Stomach

A notable contribution to the understanding of digestion was made by American army surgeon William Beaumont. Beaumont, who joined the army in 1812, was sent to a frontier post in Michigan. While there, he treated a young French-Canadian, Alexis St. Martin, who had been accidentally shot in the side.

Although St. Martin recovered, his bullet wound never fully closed and he lived with an inch-wide opening in his side that led to his stomach. Through this opening, Beaumont could not only observe changes in the stomach under varying conditions, he could remove samples of gastric juices.

Beginning in 1825, then, the army surgeon conducted more than 200 experiments and, by so doing, provided the medical world with a great deal of previously unknown information about gastric physiology (how digestive juices work) and the digestive process in a living human being.

the body's process for breaking down food, mechanically and chemically, into particles small enough to pass through the walls of the intestinal tract and into the **blood.** Once in the bloodstream, these tiny particles move throughout the body, giving nourishment.

The breaking-down process takes place in almost all parts of the digestive tract, beginning at the mouth and ending, some 15 feet later, in the anus.

In the Mouth

The digestive process starts as soon as food begins to be chewed into smaller pieces. While being chewed, the food is mixed with saliva that contains the **enzyme** ptyalin, the first of many enzymes that will help change complex and indigestible food molecules into smaller and easier-to-absorb

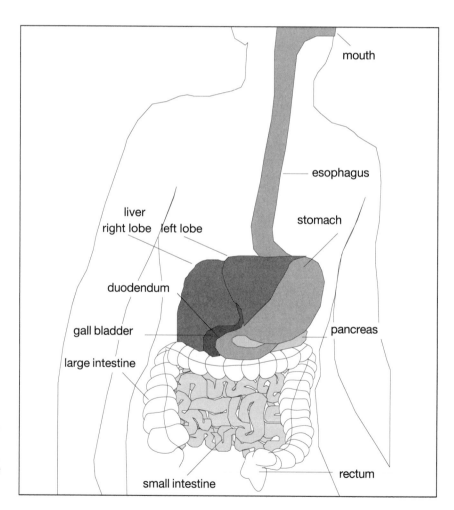

The breaking-down of food process takes place in almost all parts of the digestive tract.

ones. When in the mouth, ptyalin is already at work, converting some of the complex starches into simple sugars.

In the Stomach

After chewing, the food is swallowed and passes through the esophagus and into the stomach, where the breaking-down process goes into high gear. A strong churning motion causes the food to be thoroughly mixed with the stomach's strong digestive juices. These juices contain both **hydrochloric acid** and the enzyme pepsin. The foods are all dissolved into a thick liquid called chyme but, while the protein foods are partly digested, the other nutrients are basically unchanged.

In the Intestines

Then, in the small intestine, the digestive process is completed by a combination of pancreatic juices, containing enzymes, intestinal juices, and

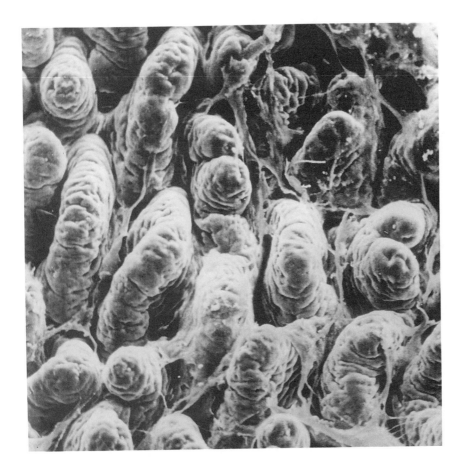

Villi on the small intestine's walls. Villi aid the absorption of nutrients.

bile. The bile, stored in the gall bladder, works primarily on the digestion and absorption of fat.

Thoroughly digested, the nutrient (food) molecules can now be absorbed by blood and lymph vessels in the small intestine's walls and carried to the body via the blood circulatory system. Undigestible food particles pass into the large intestine, where some water and minerals are absorbed and bacterial action turns the rest into feces, which are eventually eliminated as waste products.

⁎⁎ Digitizer

Digitizing tablets such as this one are commonly used in the CAD/CAM and graphics fields to create drawings, charts, or graphs and to recreate logos and other symbols.

Digitizers are computer hardware devices that change analog (continuously varying) signals into digital or electrical signals. This process allows many common measurements, such as temperature, air pressure, or engine speed, which are usually output in analog form, to be converted and used by **digital computers**.

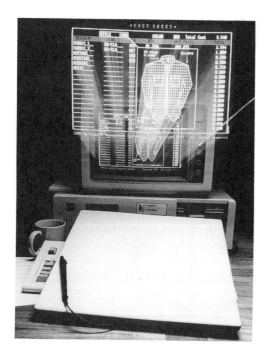

Perhaps the best known component of digitizers today is the digitizing tablet (also known as area digitizers), first developed by the RAND Corporation in 1964. Pictures can be traced on the digitizer tablet using a stylus or electric pen. The image is converted and displayed on the computer screen in digital format. Digitizing tablets are commonly used in the computer-aided design and computer-aided manufacturing (CAD/CAM) and graphics fields to create drawings, charts, or graphs and to recreate logos and other symbols.

Digitizers are also used to convert speech into a digital format. A **microphone** is used to break speech into voltages and the digitizer converts the voltages into digital code, creating words on the computer screen.

See also **Computer, industrial uses of; Computer input and output devices; Computer speech recognition**

⋆ Dishwasher

The first patent for a mechanical dishwashing device was granted in 1850 to a man named Houghton from Ogden, New York. His wooden contraption splashed water on dishes.

In 1911 the first motor-powered dishwashing appliance was developed. The first practical dishwasher for home use was marketed in 1932. Despite the fact that the average daily time spent washing dishes was 68 minutes, the machine was not in great demand. Early machines, designed for restaurants and hotels, passed dirty dishes under jets of hot water on a conveyor belt.

Modern machines operate by mechanical arms that rotate and spray hot water on dishes placed in stationary (non-moving) wire baskets. Machines draw in cold water from the sink and heat it to sterilizing temperatures. The average home dishwasher uses approximately 3.5 gallons (13.2 l) of water heated to 140° F (60° C). While that seems like a lot of water, an entire day's dishes can be washed in one load.

Josephine Cochrane, American Inventor

In 1866 Josephine Cochrane of Shelbyville, Indiana, built a dishwasher in her home. Her interest in tools to lighten household chores went beyond dishwashing machines, and she established one of the first kitchen appliance companies in America. Cochrane worked diligently on her dishwashing machine but was unable to invest enough time and money into its commercial production. After her husband's death, she began commercial production of her machine with financial help from friends.

Cochrane's first two models were both hand-operated and ultimately proved as tiring as washing dishes by hand. However, Cochrane built improved models for home and hotel use. Her larger machines were powered by a steam engine and were capable of washing hundreds of dishes in two minutes. The modern KitchenAid dishwasher is the descendant of Cochrane's early machines.

The dishwasher dries the dishes by circulating hot air. In Seattle, Washington, in 1962, Kelvinator demonstrated a dishwasher that used neither soap nor water. The machine relied on high-frequency sound waves to clean dishes but proved too costly to develop on a mass scale. This sound wave theory of cleaning showed up later in the popular science fiction TV show *Star Trek,* where the crew of the U.S.S. *Enterprise* took sonic showers.

⋆⋆ Diving apparatus

Fascination with life below the water's surface has led to the invention of diving equipment that allows exploration of the sea.

When scientists and divers study underwater environments, they equip themselves with diving gear and breathing equipment that ensure their safety. Reliable equipment, used responsibly, allows divers to remain underwater for long periods.

Diving bells, or bell-shaped hulls that are open to the water at the bottom, were one of the first devices that allowed man to descend and observe the underwater environment.

Skin divers carry no air supply but are equipped with a mask, fins, snorkel, and, in cold water, an optional wet suit. The mask allows the diver to see clearly, while the snorkel, a J-shaped breathing tube, lets the diver breathe while swimming just below the surface of the water. Fins, flat rubber shoes that resemble duck feet, provide much better propulsion than bare feet.

Scuba (an acronym for self-contained underwater breathing apparatus) diving or free diving has swimmers equipped with pressurized gas (usually compressed air) strapped onto their backs. This air supply is connected via hoses to the head gear, which includes a mask, a pressure regulator, and a mouthpiece.

Divers use weighted belts and inflatable vests to adjust their buoyancy (tendency to float) so they can descend in a gradual, controlled fashion, neither paddling furiously to get underwater nor sinking like a stone to the bottom.

When water is extremely cold, divers wear diving suits or wet suits to withstand the chill. These whole-body suits are made from a spongelike rubber material that acts as a shield against the cold water. While clinging to the body, the wet suit retains an inner layer of water, the temperature of which is regulated by the diver's body heat.

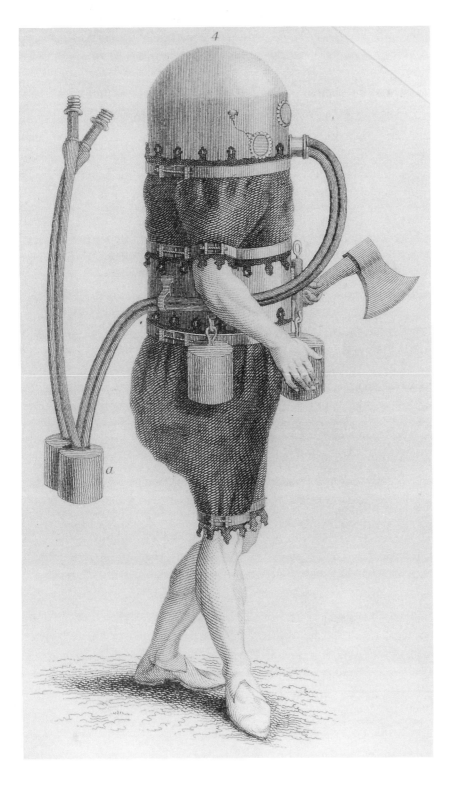

*A prototype for a
"diving machine,"
circa 1800. Reliable
equipment, used
responsibly, allows
divers to remain
underwater for long
periods.*

Tethered diving or hard-hat diving is far more complex than snorkeling or scuba diving. In this process air is pumped through a hose from the surface or an underwater structure. This approach, although more expensive, is commonly used for deep-sea excavations or to repair underwater structures such as oil rigs.

Tethered diving gear is heavy and awkward, usually consisting of a 60-pound (27 kg) helmet connected to a rubberized body suit, an 80-pound (36 kg) weighted belt, a 40-pound (18 kg) pair of weighted shoes, and a knife to cut through seaweed. The diver controls the air supply by using valves on the belt or inside the helmet.

⋆⋆ DNA (deoxyribonucleic acid)

DNA holds the key to understanding how genetic information is stored in a cell and how it is transmitted from one cell to its daughter cells.

The modern science of genetics can be traced to the research of an Austrian monk, Gregor Mendel, in the mid-1800s. Mendel developed a series of laws that described mathematically the way that inherited characteristics are passed along from one generation to the next. These laws assumed that inherited or hereditary characteristics are contained in discrete "packages" in an organism. These "packages" were called by a variety of names and eventually labeled "**gene**."

Unraveling How Heredity Works

The story of genetics during the twentieth century is, in one sense, the effort to discover more specifically what a gene is. An important breakthrough came in the early 1900s with the work of the American geneticist Thomas Hunt Morgan. Morgan bred hundreds of generations of fruit flies to study how traits are passed. Through his studies he was able to show that genes are somehow associated with the **chromosomes** that occur in the nuclei of **cells**.

By 1912 Hunt's colleague, A. H. Stirdivant, was able to construct the first chromosome "map" showing the relative positions of different genes on a chromosome. Scientists now understood that the gene had a home: it was a portion of a chromosome.

How the Information Is Carried

During the 1920s and 1930s, a small group of scientists began to look for what kind of chemical molecule a gene was made of. Most researchers assumed that genes were some kind of protein molecule. Protein molecules are large and complex and can occur in an almost infinite variety. This quality is just what one would expect for a class of molecules that must be able to carry the enormous variety of genetic traits that exist.

A smaller group of researchers looked to a second family of compounds as potential candidates for the molecules of heredity. These were the nucleic acids. Nucleic acids seemed unlikely candidates as molecules of heredity in the 1930s. What was then known about their structure suggested that they were too simple to carry the complex information needed in a molecule of heredity. Each nucleic acid molecule consists of a long chain of alternating sugar and phosphate fragments to which are attached some sequence of four or five different nitrogen bases, depending on the type of nucleic acid.

It was not clear how this relatively simple nucleic acid structure could assume enough different conformations to "code" for hundreds of thousands

DNA
(d e o x y r i b o -
n u c l e i c
a c i d)

Human DNA. Pictured is less than 0.005 percent of a complete human genome.

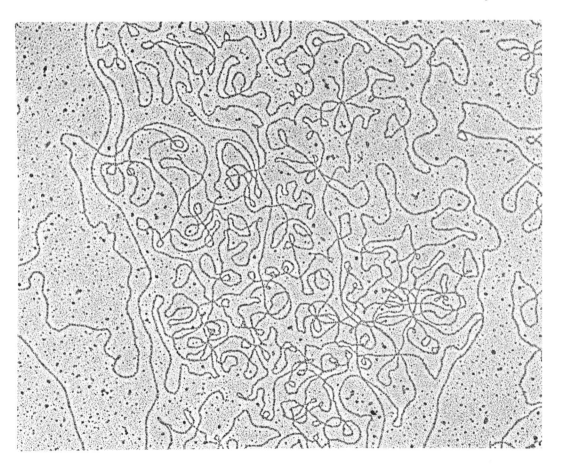

of genetic traits. In comparison, a single protein molecule contains various arrangements of 20 fundamental units (**amino acids**), making it a much better candidate as a carrier of genetic information. Yet, experimental evidence began to point to a possible role for nucleic acids in the transmission of hereditary characteristics. That evidence implicated a specific sub-family of the nucleic acids known as the deoxyribosenucleic acids, or DNA.

How Genes Arrange Themselves

As more and more experiments showed the connection between DNA and genetics, a small group of researchers in the 1940s and 1950s began to ask how a DNA molecule could code for genetic information. The two who finally resolved this question were a somewhat unusual pair, James Watson, a 24-year old American trained in genetics, and Francis Crick, a 36-year old Englishman trained in physics and self-taught in chemistry. The two met at the Cavendish Laboratories of Cambridge Uni-

James Watson and Francis Crick display their model of the DNA double helix. The pair finally resolved the question how a DNA molecule could code for genetic information.

DNA
(d e o x y r i b o -
n u c l e i c
a c i d)

RNA Is Companion Discovery

James Watson and Francis Crick had also considered what the role of DNA might be in the manufacture of proteins in a cell. The sequence that they outlined was that DNA in the nucleus of a cell might act as a template (pattern) for the formation of a second type of nucleic acid, **RNA (ribonucleic acid)**.

RNA would then leave the nucleus and itself act as a template for the production of protein. That theory, now known as the Central Dogma, has since been largely confirmed and has become a critical guiding principle of much research in molecular biology.

versity in 1951 and became instant friends. Watson and Crick were united by a common passionate belief that the structure of DNA held the key to understanding how genetic information is stored in a cell and how it is transmitted from one cell to its daughter cells.

In one sense, the challenge facing Watson and Crick was a relatively simple one. A great deal was already known about the DNA molecule. Few new discoveries were needed, but those few discoveries were crucial to solving the DNA-heredity puzzle.

First was the question of molecular architecture. How was the DNA molecule arranged so it could "hold" genetic information? The answer came when Watson saw what was essentially a "photograph" of DNA taken by a process known as X-ray crystallography.

Racing back to Cambridge after seeing this photograph, Watson convinced Crick to make an all-out attack on the DNA problem. They worked continuously for almost a week. Their approach was to construct tinker-toy-like models of the DNA molecule. They were looking for an arrangement that would give the kind of X-ray photograph that Watson had seen.

The DNA Spiral Is Born

Finally, on March 7, 1953, Watson and Crick had the answer. They built a model consisting of two helices (corkscrew-like spirals) wrapped around each other. The Watson-Crick model was a remarkable achievement, for which the two scientists won the 1954 Nobel Prize in chemistry. The molecule had exactly the shape and dimensions needed to produce the same X-ray photograph.

Watson and Crick immediately saw how the molecule could "carry" genetic information. The sequence (series) of nitrogen bases along the molecule, they said, could act as a genetic code. A sequence, such as A-T-T-C-G-C-T . . . etc., might tell a cell to make one kind of protein (such as that for red hair). Another sequence, such as G-C-T-C-T-C-G . . . etc., might code for a different kind of protein (such as that for blond hair). Watson and Crick themselves contributed to the deciphering of this genetic code although that process was long and difficult and involved the efforts of dozens of researchers over the next decade.

Scientists continue to advance their understanding of DNA. Even before the Watson-Crick discovery, they knew that DNA molecules could exist in two forms, known as "A" and "B." After the Watson-Crick discovery, two other forms known as the "C" and "D" configurations were also discovered.

In 1979, however, a fifth form of DNA known as the "Z" form was discovered by Alexander Rich and his colleagues at the Massachusetts Institute of Technology in Cambridge. The "Z" form was given its name partly because of its zig-zag shape and partly because it is so different from the more common A and B forms. The significance and role of this most recently discovered form of DNA remains a subject of research among molecular biologists.

Dog biscuit

Perhaps as many dog owners as dogs are grateful to F. H. Bennett, who invented the first dog biscuit in 1908. The biscuit began as a novelty item made from a combination of minerals, meat products, and milk.

It was the only product of the company that remained in production after the National Biscuit Company took over the Bennett bakery in 1931. The Nabisco company named the product Milk-Bone and marketed it first as a "dog's dessert" and then as a breath freshener for dogs. The Milk-Bone dog biscuit endures as one of the most popular dog treats sold in America.

Doughnut

The doughnut evolved from the round fried cakes the Dutch brought to colonial America. The doughnut form we know today is the invention of Hanson Crockett Gregory, a sea captain born in Rockport, Maine.

A popular doughnut invention story takes place on a ship. During a sea voyage, Captain Gregory and his crew struggled long and hard to guide their vessel through a ferocious storm. A thoughtful cook brought the valiant, exhausted captain a snack of fried cakes to eat as he stood at the ship's helm. When the ship suddenly encountered a huge wave, Gregory stuck his fried cake on a spoke of the wheel to free both of his hands for steering. The proud captain publicized his invention after his return to Maine, and the doughnut became a favorite treat for sailors.

Whatever their origin, doughnuts eliminated a common problem in fried cakes: the soggy center portion, which was never cooked through.

Mass Producing Doughnuts

The first doughnut-hole machine, which featured a spring-loaded tube to push the dough out of the cake's middle, was patented in 1872 by John F. Blondel of Thomaston, Maine. During World War I (1914-18), U.S. soldiers stationed in France received doughnuts from the Salvation Army, and the national fondness for the hole-less fried cakes grew. In 1921 a Bulgarian immigrant named Arnold Levitt invented a machine that could mass-produce doughnuts. His Donut Corporation of America, founded just after World War II (1939-45), helped bring the doughnut worldwide acclaim. By the end of the 1980s, America's two most famous doughnut makers, Dunkin' Donuts and Mister Donut, had 1,878 and 558 franchises, respectively. Today the word "doughnut" embraces a huge variety of powdered, glazed, frosted, and plain shapes that are sticks as well as circles with holes.

Chief High Eagle of the Wampanoag tribe claimed his own people invented the doughnut when a wayward arrow missed a Pilgrim homemaker and pierced her fried cake instead.

⋆ Dry cleaning

Many fabrics such as cotton and linen can be washed in water. Garments made of these cloths can be water cleaned without shrinking or the dye running. Some fabrics, however, cannot be water cleaned.

As a profession, dry cleaning dates back to Mycenean (Greek) civilization, around 1600 B.C. Archaeologists believe these ancient dry cleaners used absorbent earth or powdered meal to draw sweat, odors, and soil from clothing.

Since the eighteenth century, people have protected fabrics from shrinkage and warpage by replacing water-based cleaners with chemical substitutes such as naphtha, benzine, and benzol. Other products, such as pinene and camphene, successfully removed spots. A common home dry

One technique involved the vigorous application of grated potatoes as a means of cleaning unwashable materials, furniture, and even oil paintings.

Which Chemicals Work?

Various legends describe how chemical solvents came to light. Some credit a maid who spilled turpentine on a soiled dress. Another version describes a French sailor who fell into a barrel of turpentine and came out with a spotless uniform.

In 1845 Parisian dyer Jean-Baptiste Jolly spilled kerosene on a soiled tablecloth and discovered that the substance cleaned the spot. He coined the term "dry cleaning" to differentiate it from regular soap and water wash. His firm, Jolly-Belin, became Europe's first professional dry cleaner.

By 1897 Ludwig Anthelin of Leipzig, Germany, discovered that application of carbon tetrachloride gave acceptable results without creating a fire hazard. Because the solution was an irritant, fans to ventilate solvent storage chambers were necessary to protect workers from developing breathing problems.

From 1921 to 1925, cleaners searched for a safe, nonflammable solvent. Around 1930 dry cleaners introduced a less harmful chemical named Stoddard solvent to honor W. J. Stoddard, president of the National Institute of Drycleaning. Other nonflammable synthetic solvents were compounded, especially trichloroethylene and perchloroethylene, and were used both in professional cleaning plants and coin-operated machines.

cleaning method called for the application of **gasoline** to dirty clothes to dissolve protein and fatty or oily substances, such as blood or gravy stains, but the flammability of gasoline proved hazardous.

By the mid-1800s, small businesses specializing in formal dry cleaning had opened. Valet shops and pressing clubs became attachments to laundries, where a variety of services, including alterations, reweaving, and repairs, led to full-time clothing care. By 1919 dry cleaning was a $55 million industry. A half-century later, the industry had grown to a $2.8 billion enterprise.

How Clothes Are Dry Cleaned

In dry cleaning, clothes are inspected, tagged, and then sorted as to color, fiber, and weave. Delicate fabrics—such as cashmere and angora wool, ornate lace, leather, suede, fur, and other fragile materials—and seriously stained garments are spot-cleaned by hand. Decorations, belts, lace collars and cuffs, fur pieces, and shoulder pads are removed for individualized care.

The bulk of the soiled clothes are churned in a large drum similar to a **washing machine**. As they tumble through mists of solvent and detergent, the dirt is loosened. Then the bundle undergoes a second cycle to agitate and remove the chemical cleaning agent.

Used solvent is filtered or distilled to remove soil and to allow the reuse of the chemicals. To complete the job, a spotter brushes and steamguns stubborn spots. Finally, the clothing is dried. Pressers then shape and steam garments with a professional-sized iron or over a basket-shaped hoop.

African American tailor and abolitionist Thomas L. Jennings (1791-1859) patented a dry-cleaning process in 1821.

In 1960 permanent-press materials introduced the public to the ease and low cost of wash-and-wear clothing, creating less demand for professional cleaning. A second blow to the industry was the environmental movement, which urged city councils to regulate or ban the release of possibly harmful solvents into the atmosphere.

⋆⋆ Dynamite

Dynamite is an explosive that was invented in 1866 by Swedish physicist Alfred Nobel and patented by him a year later. Nobel is most familiar to us today as the founder of the Nobel prizes. The prizes were Nobel's way of atoning for the destructive force he had unleashed with his invention. He left his multimillion-dollar fortune, made by the patenting and manufacture of dynamite and other inventions, to establish prizes awarded "to those, who during the preceding year, shall have conferred the greatest benefit on mankind."

Nobel the Pacifist

Actually, Nobel invented dynamite to make the dangerous explosive nitroglycerin a safer substance. Nobel was a pacifist, a person who opposes war or any kind of violence. As a pacifist, he did not intend his invention to be used for war. He believed its use could bring war to an end more swiftly, or that the horrors of such an explosive would prevent warfare in the first place.

Nobel also saw the need for explosives in mining, engineering, industry, transport, and other peaceful uses. With dynamite, Nobel made possible many of the great engineering projects of the nineteenth and twentieth centuries.

Making Nitroglycerin Safer

For centuries prior to the introduction of dynamite, gunpowder was the only explosive available. It was useful but limited in its applications. Then in 1846, an Italian chemist named Ascanio Sobrero (1812-1888) invented nitroglycerin. The pale-yellow oil was not detonated (set off) by flame or spark like gunpowder, but by impact, or percussion. Unfortunately, it was so highly combustible that if even a small bottle were dropped, it could easily blow up a building.

In the mid-nineteenth century, Nobel and his father Immanuel, also a noted inventor, became convinced of nitroglycerin's promise and began manufacturing it. They encountered the same problems with its combustibility. In fact, Nobel's own factory blew up in 1864, killing five people, including his younger brother. Many unfortunate experiences involving the inappropriate use of nitroglycerin were reported. Not realizing that even a slight shock or temperature change could cause the oil to explode, people reportedly used nitroglycerin for lamp oil, boot polish, or for greasing wagon wheels—often with fatal consequences.

Despite the enormous risks associated with transporting nitroglycerin, miners were particularly anxious to get their hands on it. As manufacturers struggled to keep up with the demand for nitroglycerin, the number of explosions during the transportation process increased. Many warehouses, factories, and ships around the world were damaged or destroyed, which created a worldwide stir. Governments, pressured by public outcry, began to ban the transport and/or possession of the material.

The need for a safe but powerful explosive prompted Nobel to find a way to make nitroglycerin safer without significantly decreasing its power. He had already invented (in 1865) a detonating cap to give more control over the timing of an explosion once the substance was in place. But the cap did not solve the problem of handling or transportation.

Nobel then discovered that he could turn the oil into a manageable solid by soaking it up into a porous material. Many nonexplosive inert substances were tried: paper, wood, waste, **brick** dust, and dry clay. Finally in 1864, he discovered a mineral called kieselguhr, found mainly in northern Germany, that seemed to do the job. It soaked up the nitroglycerin without changing its chemical makeup, and the resulting doughlike substance could be made into hard cakes or sticks. Though it was 25 percent less

Alfred Nobel, a pacifist, was horrified at the eagerness of governments to use dynamite in war material. He created the Nobel prizes to offset the damage done by his invention.

powerful than pure nitroglycerin, it was still far more powerful than gun-powder, and easily manageable. Nobel named this new explosive "dyna-mite" (after the Greek word *dynamis,* meaning "power"). He patented it under two names: Dynamite and Nobel's Safety Powder.

Dynamite Hits the Streets

Even in this safer form, dynamite was at first regarded suspiciously by some governments, which refused to allow its importation. The major gunpowder manufacturers, afraid it would cut into their business, tried to stop it from being patented. Later, when the military uses of dynamite became apparent, governments reversed their decision. Soon Nobel had factories worldwide.

Within 20 years of the patent, 66,500 tons of dynamite were pro-duced worldwide. Ninety years after its invention, 400,000 tons a year were produced in the United States alone. Well into the twentieth century, dynamite was essential in warfare. The explosive power of bombs used in World War II (1939-45) was made possible by Nobel's inventions.

⋆⋆ Earthquake

An earthquake is an unpredictable event in which masses of rock shift below the earth's surface, releasing enormous amounts of energy and sending out shock waves that sometimes cause the ground to shake dramatically. Not all earthquakes are enormous, but they are one of the earth's most destructive forces. Entire structures, including houses and dams, have been known to collapse in an earthquake.

Why the Earth Trembles

The earth's crust is made up of many plates that constantly move. Occasionally the plates bump against each other along the places where they meet, called fault lines. The movement of one of these immense plates can shift great masses of weight and pressure onto other weaker layers. When this pressure gives way, an earthquake can take place.

Measuring the Quake

An earthquake's power can be measured in two ways: by intensity (strength) and magnitude (ground covered). While intensity of a quake is usually described through people's perceptions and the amount of buildings destroyed, magnitude is measured by using seismographs or devices that detect ground movement. These magnitude measurements also allow scientists to precisely compare earthquakes around the world.

People were experiencing and describing the effects of earthquakes long before scientific measuring devices were available. But intensities

Earth tremors are almost always occurring within the earth. It is estimated that as many as one million earthquakes take place every year. Fortunately, most are of low intensity.

were more formally rated in the late 1800s and later refined around 1930 when the United States adopted and revised an early European version called the Mercalli scale. Today seismologists use the Richter scale. (For a complete discussion of these methods, see **Earthquake measurement scale.**)

Readings from seismographic stations provide scientists with information about the location of the earthquake's epicenter or origin. From the epicenter, shock waves travel outward in the same way that rings of water ripple out in a pond when a pebble is dropped.

Although earthquakes cannot be predicted, keeping accurate records of their intensity and magnitude helps scientists discover where earth tremors happen repeatedly. In the United States, many populated areas such as San Francisco are located along fault lines. This requires that structures be built with special support to help them withstand intense ground shaking.

See also **Earthquake measurement scale; Earthquake-proofing techniques**

A National Guardsman walks past the remains of a three-story apartment complex in San Francisco after an earthquake rocked the area on October 17, 1989. Earthquakes are one of the earth's most destructive forces.

⋆⋆ Earthquake measurement scale

The earliest **earthquake** measurements were simple descriptions called intensity ratings. The results could be unreliable depending on the distance between the quake's source (epicenter) and the people evaluating the event.

A more systematic approach was developed by an Italian seismologist, Guiseppe Mercalli, in 1902. A seismologist is a scientist who studies earthquakes and their causes. Mercalli judged earthquake intensity by measuring the damage done to buildings. The United States Coast and Geodetic Survey adapted his method, which they called the modified Mercalli scale. The measurements were divided into 12 categories: level 2 was "felt by persons at rest," but at level 7 it was "difficult to

On the Richter scale, an earthquake measuring 8 can level a city.

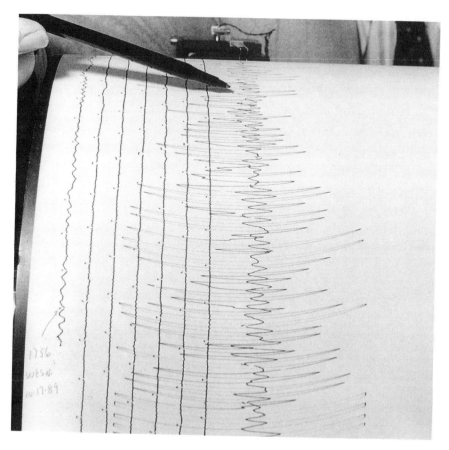

The seismogram of the October 17, 1989, earthquake that shook San Francisco.

On the Richter scale, each whole number increase means that the magnitude of the quake is 10 times greater than the previous whole number.

stand." Level 10 caused most buildings to collapse, and level 12, the most intense, combined ground fissures with tsunamis (tidal waves) and almost total destruction.

Richter Scale

But seismologists needed a way to determine the size, or magnitude, of an earthquake. The measurement would compare the strength of earthquakes in a meaningful way, not merely compare damage as Mercalli's method did. The measurement was invented in 1935 by American seismologist Charles F. Richter, a professor of seismology at the California Institute of Technology in Pasadena. Richter's system of measurement, called the Richter scale, was based on his studies of earthquakes in southern California. It has become the most widely used assessment of earthquake severity in the world.

Richter measured ground movement with a seismograph, compared the reading to others taken at various distances from the epicenter, then calculated an average magnitude from all reports. The results are plotted on a scale. Each whole number increase means that the magnitude of the quake is 10 times greater than the previous whole number. Thus, an earthquake with a magnitude of 6.5 has 10 times the force of one with a magnitude of 5.5 and so on.

The amount of energy an earthquake releases is calculated in a different manner. Instead of tenfold jumps with each increase in magnitude, energy released is measured in roughly thirtyfold increments. Thus, an earthquake with a value of 7 releases 30 times the amount of energy as an earthquake measured at 6, while an earthquake of 8 would have 900 times the energy as one valued at 6.

Today the modified Mercalli scale is used in combination with the Richter scale because both methods are helpful in gauging the total impact of an earthquake.

⋆⋆ Earthquake-proofing techniques

Earthquakes occur in many parts of the world, sometimes over and over again. The size of a quake is measured by points on the Richter seismic scale, while the strength of a quake is measured in terms of damage and lives lost. The damage and casualties depend on population density and the quality of building construction.

In the San Francisco earthquake of 1906, a majority of the buildings withstood the tremors but were destroyed by the fire that followed. The quake not only brought public demands for fireproofing techniques, but for earthquake-proof primary and secondary water supply systems for fighting fires.

Engineering and Materials

During later earthquakes, many overpasses of the California interstate highway system collapsed or were damaged because of their inflexible (stiff) design. In the 1950s, the concept of ductility, or pliancy, was formulated. It called for the use of energy-absorbing features and reinforced building materials.

The major thrust of earthquake-proofing by architects is to prevent the collapse of buildings. The ability of a building to withstand the stress of an earthquake depends upon its type of construction, shape, mass distribution, and rigidity. Various combinations of techniques are used.

The collapse of the Nimitz Freeway in Oakland during the San Francisco earthquake on October 17, 1989, made it clear that not enough had been done to prevent damage to roads, buildings, and other structures in case of earthquake.

Square, rectangular, or shell-shaped buildings and buildings with few stories can withstand vibrations better than L-shaped structures or skyscrapers. To reduce stress, a building's ground floor can be supported by very rigid, hollow columns, while the rest of the building is supported by flexible columns located inside the hollow columns. Another method is to use rollers or rubber pads to separate the foundation columns from the ground.

To help prevent collapse, roofs can be made of lightweight materials. Exterior walls can be made more durable by strengthening them with steel or wooden beams or with concrete reinforced with iron rods. Flexible window frames can hold windows in place during tremors.

Some architectural ideas are not tested until an earthquake occurs. The San Fernando earthquake of 1971 taught engineers a valuable lesson. The so-called soft story concept failed completely. It was thought that the upper stories of a high-rise building would suffer less damage if the first story were allowed to flex, having windows and facades instead of rigid walls and columns. Many of these buildings collapsed.

The collapse of the Nimitz Freeway in nearby Oakland during the San Francisco earthquake of 1989 made it clear that despite extensive research and building codes for resistant construction, not enough had actually been done to prevent damage.

See also **Earthquake measurement scale**

⋆⋆ Earth's core

Earth itself is a huge magnet.

If one were to drill a hole into the earth, after about 4,000 miles (6,452 km) the bit would reach the earth's center, or core. First the drill would bore through the earth's crust, composed of cool solid rock. Next would come the mantle. Next is the outer core of hot molten or liquid iron. Finally the drill would reach the earth's center or inner core, which is solid. Unlike the rock of the **earth's mantle** and crust, the earth's core is thought to be entirely metal, composed largely of nickel and **iron**.

Seismology Contributes Information

The earth's innermost layer was a complete mystery before the development of the science of **seismology** and seismic instruments. Seismology is the study of **earthquakes** and their causes.

Around 1900 a discovery by the Irish scientist Richard Dixon Oldham provided more clues about the earth's core. He found that tremors or waves resulting from explosions or earthquakes travel through the interior of the earth in different directions and speeds. He called them P (for primary) and S (for secondary) waves.

These discoveries of seismic shock waves helped scientists better understand the composition of the earth's interior. By the mid-1920s, they realized that some waves could not penetrate through the core of the earth.

These seismic waves also help scientists learn the different degrees of rigidity (stiffness) of the earth's many layers. They saw that as primary shock waves move through the earth, the speed of the waves generally increases with their depth. While shock waves travel through the earth's crust at four miles (6.4 km) per second, they reach seven miles (11.3 km) per second at the center of the earth. When the shock waves suddenly shift in direction and speed, scientists are able to detect at what distances the earth's various layers are located.

Oldham's work, which included a suggestion of a thin outer crust, helped other scientists accurately map the earth's different layers. In 1909

The earth's various layers. The earth's core is thought to be entirely metal, composed largely of nickel and iron.

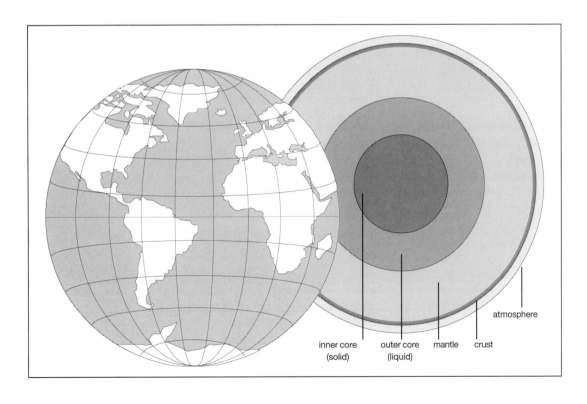

inner core (solid) outer core (liquid) mantle crust atmosphere

Andrija Mohorovicic (1857-1936) published important findings from his study of an earthquake that hit Croatia in Eastern Europe. Mohorovicic was able to calculate the depth of the boundary where material changes from the earth's crust to its mantle. This important discovery earned him the name for which that boundary is now entitled, called the **Mohorovicic discontinuity**, or the Moho.

See also **Earth's mantle**

⋆˙⋆ Earth's magnetic field

Some scientists have suggested that a period of strong solar-flare activity could wipe out the Earth's magnetic field.

Earth's magnetic field, though observed by humans for centuries, has been explained only recently by science. Most of the field is the result of electricity flowing through the molten metal outer core of Earth as it rotates. The remainder is caused by the interaction of the main magnetic field and the **solar wind** and by electric currents in the **ionosphere**. As a result of the magnetic field, Earth acts like a permanent bar magnet with its poles tilted 11 degrees away from its axis of rotation.

Magnetism is a force that appears repeatedly in and around Earth. Magnetic declination is the name of the phenomenon that marks a distinction between true north and magnetic north. Magnetic dip describes the fact that freely suspended compass needles dip downward with increased northward latitude.

Magnetism is so common that compass needles are affected by displays of the *aurora borealis* (northern lights), time of day or year, and by their own geographical location.

Scientists have determined that Earth itself is a magnet, with variations in declination and dip caused by geo-electric currents and short-term variations from electric charges in the atmosphere.

In the early 1960s, a detailed study of paleomagnetism was published, indicating nine major reversals in the past 3.6 million years. Today it is accepted that Earth's magnetic field can exist in "normal" and "reversed" states, with a transition period of 2,000 to 10,000 years to change polarity.

More evidence was presented in 1965 by Richard Doell and Brent Dalrymple. They gave a complete picture of reversals over the previous five million years, linking the reversals worldwide. Their work also supported arguments for **continental drift** and **plate tectonics**.

Some scientists have suggested that a period of strong solar-flare activity could wipe out the Earth's magnetic field. At the conclusion of the activity, a machine called a magnetohydrodynamic dynamo could restore the magnetic field, but it would be reversed.

During the twentieth century, scientists have noticed a steady reduction of about 6 percent in the strength of the magnetic field. Should this continue, the magnetic field will be gone in only 1,500 years. Some scientists believe this is only a fluctuation, and that it will recover its strength in time. Others believe it indicates a reversal on its way.

See also **Compass**

⋆⋆ Earth's mantle

In the early 1900s, scientists were fairly certain that the earth was made up of many layers, like an onion, but they did not know exactly where the layers started and ended. In 1909 Andrija Mohorovicic (1857-1936), a Croatian (Eastern European) seismologist, helped reveal the existence of a second layer inside the earth, which is called the earth's mantle. (Seismology is the study of earthquakes and their causes.) Beneath the mantle lies the innermost layer, the **earth's core**.

Mohorovicic studied Yugoslavian **earthquake** records, which showed that two different sets of earth shock waves were sent out from a single earthquake. Because the second set of waves exactly mirrored the first set, Mohorovicic concluded that the additional set was actually the first bouncing back from a resistant surface, or a layer of different material inside the earth. This resistant surface, or discontinuity, allowed Mohorovicic to guess the existence of a second layer of material just inside the crust. From that discovery, the boundary where the crust and the mantle meet is now referred to as the **Mohorovicic discontinuity**, or Moho.

Mohorovicic also noticed from these experiments that the waves, or tremors, traveled at different speeds depending on the thickness of the material inside the earth. This information helped scientists map out the different types of rock in areas where drilling was impossible. For example, the lowest level of the crust that rests next to the mantle is composed of basaltic rock.

After the Moho was discovered, scientists were able to plot these Earth waves on sensitive shock recording devices called seismographs. From this information, we know that the mantle is approximately 1,798 miles (2,900 km) thick, making up about 45 percent of the earth's radius.

Similar to the earth's uneven crust, the earth's mantle is thought to be irregular. The unevenness is mostly caused by enormous pressures inside the earth, which force the weaker areas of the rocky sub-layers out of alignment. When the weaker sub-layers, or plates, give way to pressure or stronger plates, earthquakes result.

Ever since the discovery of the mantle, scientists have wanted to probe into the physical nature of the earth's inner layer. And because the mantle layer resides so much closer to the surface of the ocean, there were plans in the late 1950s to drill into the Moho from floating platforms out at sea. But after a number of test drillings, funding was withdrawn and the project—Project Mohole—was abandoned in the mid-1960s.

Even today, information about the composition of the mantle comes from the study of earthquakes and shock waves. Because waves travel at different speeds, depending upon the density of the rock, seismologists can guess what materials are contained within the mantle.

Three different types of rock make up the mantle, including two primary rocks, peridotite and eclogite, and a third lesser-known rock, kimberlite. Eclogite resembles basalt, the lava that people associate with volcanoes. It is possible that eclogite transforms into lava as pressures shift within the mantle and volcanoes result.

See also **Earth's core**

⋆⋆ Earth survey satellite

Before the space age, scientists generally believed that few details of Earth's surface could be seen from altitudes above 100 miles (161 km). Astronaut Gordon Cooper shattered that idea when he reported seeing roads, buildings, and even smoke from chimneys during his flight in a *Mercury* capsule in May 1963.

Later observations used high-technology cameras to detect small variations of energy on Earth's surface. Using these photos of energy emissions, plants could be distinguished from rock, soil, or water. It was easy to tell the difference between healthy and diseased crops, healthy or poor soil conditions, wet or dry soil, and even various crops under cultivation.

Landsats View Earth

The first satellites to carry out detailed observations of Earth were the *Landsats* developed by General Electric for NASA (the National Aeronautics and Space Administration). First launched in 1972, they orbited about 500 miles (805 km) above Earth, sending back pictures of its entire surface. The early satellites could see features no smaller than one acre, but *Landsat 4* was able to narrow this down to one-fifth acre (about two city lots). This satellite was built for retrieval by a **space shuttle** so it could be repaired and reused.

Landsat satellites have yielded valuable data for a wide variety of fields. Cartographers (mapmakers) have used them to chart normally inac-

A Landsat 5 photo of the power plant at Chernobyl, Ukraine, after its nuclear reactor exploded in April 1986. Landsat satellites have yielded valuable data for a wide variety of fields.

cessible areas. Environmentalists have used them to track air pollution and oil spills and to study the ozone layer. *Landsat* photos have helped the agriculture industry better manage crop and timber resources by revealing when to plant and harvest for maximum yield and giving advanced warning of drought. The satellites also help shipping companies determine the flow of ice in arctic regions.

Overall, the largest purchasers of *Landsat* data have been the oil and mining industries. Large folds and ruptures of Earth's surface, as well as certain colors, can indicate the location of mineral and shale deposits.

Seasat Explores the Ocean

In addition to *Landsat,* oceanographers benefited greatly from *Seasat 1.* This survey satellite, launched in 1978, can tell sea-surface temperature, wind speed, wind direction, and the amount of water in the atmosphere. These satellites also help find sea currents, information useful for fishing fleets and shipping companies who want to route their tankers to save fuel.

Albert Einstein revolutionized our view of the universe and helped us better understand the nature of the physical world.

⋆* Einstein, Albert

German-Swiss-American physicist Albert Einstein (1879-1955) was one of the geniuses of the twentieth century and one of the greatest scientists of all time. He revolutionized our view of the universe with his theory of relativity and helped us better understand the nature of the physical world, including time, space, gravity, light, and magnetism.

Einstein was born in Ulm, Germany, the son of an engineer. As a boy he moved with his family to Milan, Italy, and devoted his time to the study of mathematics. In six months, he taught himself calculus, an advanced type of algebra. But Einstein lacked the patience to study subjects in which he had no interest and soon left school.

In 1895 Einstein traveled to Zurich to take the entrance examination at the Swiss Polytechnique Institute, where a high school degree was not required. He failed the exam but, after a year of outside study, he retook and passed the exam.

Four years later, Einstein received his degree from the Institute. He had not been a particularly good student and is said to have been graduated only because of the help he received from his fellow students' lecture notes. After graduation, Einstein had problems finding a job, partly because of his academic record, partly because he was not a Swiss citizen, and partly because he was Jewish.

Then, in 1901, Einstein received an appointment at the Swiss Patent Office. The job was not particularly demanding, and Einstein had plenty of time to study on his own. In addition, the job allowed him to apply for Swiss citizenship. During the seven years that he worked at the Patent Office, Einstein was able to complete the work necessary for his doctorate at the University of Zurich and to write three of the most significant papers in the history of science.

Einstein's first paper offered mathematical equations that supported a phenomenon called Brownian movement, which dealt with the movement of solid particles in fluid, and allowed for the calculation of mass of a single atom. His second paper offered mathematical support for photoelectric effect, which combines light and energy. It was especially for the development of this law that Einstein was awarded the Nobel Prize for physics in 1921.

Theory of Relativity

Einstein's most far-reaching accomplishment of 1905 may well have been his third paper, dealing with the development of **relativity** theories. In this paper, Einstein suggested a new way of looking at the universe, the first real break in physical thought since the time of **Isaac Newton**.

In the paper and with later research, Einstein showed mathematically that light is the fastest thing in the universe. Einstein also proposed that time would slow down, that length would shorten, and that mass would increase once a traveler neared the speed of light. His relation between time and space is called the time-space continuum.

In spite of the importance of his 1905 work, Einstein was unable to get an academic appointment until four years later, when he became

*Einstein's
objective was to
find a single set
of equations
that would
describe all
physical
phenomena.*

associate professor of theoretical physics at the University of Zurich. But his star began to rise quickly after that. In 1911 he was appointed to the chair of physics at the German University in Prague, Czechoslovakia. A year later he returned to the Swiss Polytechnique Institute in Zurich. Finally, in 1914, a position was created specifically for him at the Kaiser Wilhelm Physical Institute in Berlin, Germany. He remained in that position until 1932.

In a turn of circumstances, Einstein had been coming to the United States as visiting professor at the California Institute of Technology (Cal Tech), in Pasadena in the early 1930s. When Adolf Hitler came to power in Germany during Einstein's third visit to Cal Tech, he decided not to return to Berlin. Instead, he accepted an appointment at the Princeton Institute for Advanced Studies in New Jersey, where he remained until his death. He became an American citizen in 1940.

Einstein's other areas of study included the gravitational effect of the Sun, solar energy, and solar flares. He showed mathematically that the Sun's activity has an effect on **Earth's magnetic field.** Einstein also showed how black holes could exist in the universe and how they act as gravity wells. Today scientists believe that time may stand still within black holes.

Einstein's major interest during the final decades of his life was a search for a unification theory that would combine gravitational and electromagnetic theories. His objective was to find a single set of equations that would describe all physical phenomena. He was unsuccessful in that effort, as have been all scientists since his time.

International Fame

In 1940 Einstein became involved in a political debate over the use of **nuclear fission** for the production of an **atomic bomb.** Scientists, fearing that Hitler might develop a bomb first, recruited Einstein to help them. He had no particular interest or expertise in the subject of nuclear fission. But he was the world's best-known scientist and, therefore, the person most likely to make the needed impact on political leaders. So, he was asked to sign a letter, written by other nuclear scientists, addressed to U.S. president Franklin D. Roosevelt.

The letter described progress in the field of nuclear fission and the potential of that research for weapons development. Largely as a result of that letter, the United States embarked on the Manhattan Project, a program that resulted in the production of the world's first nuclear weapons. Throughout his life, Einstein held strong pacifist views. During World War I (1914-18), he opposed Germany's attacks on Russia, France, and other countries. He refused to participate in war-related research that was expected of college professors during the war. Only his Swiss citizenship protected him from retribution for his "unpatriotic" views and acts.

Hitler's rise to power convinced Einstein that war was sometimes necessary, and he reluctantly supported the Allied (United States, England, and France) effort against Germany in World War II (1939-45). At the conclusion of the war, however, he renewed his support for pacifist, one-world, and antinuclear causes. In addition, he was active in Jewish causes and, in 1952, was asked to become president of the newly created state of Israel. He declined the offer, explaining that he did not have the right personality for the job and wished to have uninterrupted time to work on scientific ideas.

Einstein died in Princeton, New Jersey, on April 18, 1955.

See also **Electromagnetism; Quantum theory; Relativity**

Einsteinium

The discovery of element 99 was shrouded in mystery. The first scientific papers describing its properties appeared in 1954 and indicated that additional information was available about the element, but that this information could not be released.

Eventually the reason for this secrecy was explained. The element had been discovered among the products of the first fusion (nuclear) bomb experiment conducted at Bikini Atoll in the Pacific Ocean in November 1952. The element's existence was later confirmed through experiments at the Oak Ridge National Laboratories in Tennessee. The element was named "einsteinium," after **Albert Einstein**. The element's chemical symbol is Es. Although microgram quantities of the element have been prepared, no uses for it have yet been suggested.

See also **Nuclear fission**

✦ Elasticity

Just about every solid material possesses some degree of elasticity, and so do most liquids. Some common highly elastic products are rubber bands, kitchen spatulas, and bicycle tires. Even buildings and bridges have some degree of elasticity (or give) so they can adjust to small shifts in the earth's surface.

Chemical Principles

Elasticity is a chemical property that allows a solid body to return to its original shape after an outside force is removed. The key to determining whether a substance is elastic is to apply a force to it. With sufficient force, the substance should change its size, shape, or volume. If, when the force is removed, the sample returns to its original state, then it is elastic.

Elasticity is a chemical property that allows a solid body to return to its original shape after an outside force is removed.

Bicycle tires, rubber bands, and kitchen spatulas are some common highly elastic products.

If the substance returns only partially (or not at all) to its original state, it is called inelastic.

If too much force is applied, the material is in danger of reaching its elastic limit. The elastic limit is the point at which the material is bent beyond its ability to return to its original shape. Once the elastic limit is passed, the material will experience permanent reshaping, called plastic deformation, and will no longer act as an elastic substance.

This stretching/recoiling activity is easily seen by hanging a weight from a spring: if the weight is within the spring's elastic capacity, the spring will bounce back (in an elastic manner). However, if the weight is too heavy for the spring, the weight will pull the spring straight, making it inelastic. (Think of a **Slinky,** the coiled wire toy that travels down stairs and then regains its original shape. If too much force is applied to it, the slinky becomes bent out of shape or inelastic.)

Elasticity works because of two basic forces that operate at the molecular level: attracting force and repelling force.

Elasticity works because of two basic forces that operate at the molecular level: attracting force and repelling force. When at rest, these forces within the molecules balance each other. By adding a compressing force (say, by squeezing a spring), the repelling force increases in an attempt to once again balance the system. Likewise, by adding a stretching force (as in a weight pulling a spring), the attracting force increases, causing the elastic material to bounce back.

Early Experiments

The first scientist to conduct in-depth research into the behavior of elastic materials was the famous English physicist Robert Hooke (1635-1703). Through experiments Hooke discovered that the relationship between tension (the force applied) and extension (the amount of bending that is produced) is directly proportional. For example, a weight will stretch a spring, and a weight twice as heavy will stretch it twice as much. Hooke's research has since been combined into a series of mathematical principles known as Hooke's law.

More than 100 years after Hooke's studies, another English scientist, Thomas Young, discovered that different elastic materials bend to different degrees when a force is applied. For example, brass bends more than lead, but less than rubber. The amount of elasticity of a particular material, Young found, can be expressed as a constant called Young's modulus. Knowledge of Young's modulus is essential to modern architects, who must be able to predict how construction materials will act when they are under stress.

*⋆ Electric arc

The discovery of electricity in the late 1700s had a momentous impact on all branches of science. In early experiments, researchers explored the behavior of sparks and electric current. Eventually, Italian physicist Alessandro Volta built what was then called a "pile" of electrical cells—essentially a battery—that was capable of producing a strong current. It was this invention that led to the discovery of the electric arc.

Scientists around the world soon began assembling larger batteries, but British chemist Sir Humphry Davy was the first to concentrate on the arc produced between the two electrodes of a battery. When the electrodes are separated, a strong electric current will leap across the space from one electrode to the other, producing a curve of intense light and heat. The current is conducted by gases in the air surrounding the electrodes. Davy first noticed that the arc could be improved by using **carbon** electrodes instead of metal.

Electric Light Is Born

Arc lights are used as spotlights, where a tremendous amount of focused light is needed.

This discovery gave birth to the entire field of electric lighting. From 1805 onwards, Davy and other scientists demonstrated the electric arc to the public. The brilliant light it produced was impressive, but the commercial use of arc lamps was delayed until cheaper sources of power were invented in the late 1800s.

When interest in the electric arc as a source of light revived, basic research on the nature of the arc also resumed. At the time, electric arcs often became unstable, causing them to hiss and sputter. In 1899 a British electrical engineer named Hertha Ayrton solved this baffling problem, which was caused by oxidation of carbon from the positive electrode. Her discovery suggested changes in the way electrodes were manufactured, leading to greater arc stability and more effective lighting. As a result, Ayrton was elected the first woman member of the Institution of Electrical Engineers.

Today the electric arc remains useful as a source of light and heat in many special applications such as arc welding, movie filming and projection, and testing of aerospace materials.

★·* Electric blanket

The forerunner of the modern electric blanket was designed in 1912 by American physician Sidney Russell, who was trying to create an effective heating pad for his patients. Russell found that he could produce the desired heat by passing an electrical current through insulated metal tape that had been secured inside a blanket covering.

It was not until the 1930s, however, that the electric blanket was commercially developed in the United States.

Safety was a major concern in electric blanket use. Research conducted during World War II (1939-45) on electrically heated uniforms for airplane pilots led to some safety improvements to electric blankets. The most important was the addition of protective **vinyl** coverings for the electrical elements (wires and plugs). In 1967, after a series of accidents, a U.S. company called Dreamland built in a monitoring system that cuts off electricity to the blanket if it overheats. In 1970 Britain's Thermega marketed a blanket that replaced the electrical elements with tubes carrying hot water.

★·* Electric charge

The concept of electric charges goes back more than 2,000 years to the ancient Greeks. Their word for amber, a resin that had the ability to hold a static electric charge, was *elektron,* from which the word "electricity" is derived.

In more recent times, electric charge was studied by Stephen Gray. In 1729 he discovered that rubbing a glass tube created an electric charge that was "conducted" through the tube and into corks at either end. Four years later, French physicist Charles Du Fay experimented with Gray's concept of conduction and found that twine was an excellent conductor if it were damp. If the twine were dry it inhibited the electric charge and acted instead as an insulator.

Ben Franklin's Contribution

Great advances in the understanding of electric charge came from the work of American diplomat and inventor Benjamin Franklin. Franklin did, indeed, fly a kite in a lightning storm and was able to draw an electric charge out of the sky and store the charge in a Leyden jar, a type of electrical condenser. He also invented the lightning rod to conduct an electric charge safely into the ground, thereby protecting buildings from lightning strikes and fire.

Franklin also investigated the two different electric charges and came to the conclusion that electricity was a fluid that existed as either an "excess" or a "deficiency" in an object. Two objects with identical charges repelled each other, but an object with an excess charge attracted an object that had a deficiency. Upon contact the charges would balance out. Franklin concluded that electricity flowed from a positive object (with an excess charge) to a negative one (with a deficient charge). This was a daring but incorrect conclusion.

In 1897 Joseph J. Thomson discovered a **subatomic particle** that was named the "**electron**." It was discovered that the flow of electricity was related to electrons that carried a negative charge. In addition, the electron traveled from a negatively charged object to one that was positively charged.

Though Franklin's concept was consistently incorrect, it made no difference to the experiments and their results. Franklin is responsible for and deserves the credit for establishing the modern concept of positive and negative electric charges.

See also **Electromagnetism**

⋆⋆ Electrocardiograph (ECG)

In the late 1700s, medical researchers learned that muscles produce tiny electric pulses. They reasoned that a recording of the electric impulses of the heart could reveal irregularities and, hence, heart disease. Next researchers tried to develop accurate ways to measure the heart's impulses.

In 1903 Dutch physiologist Willem Einthoven introduced his string galvanometer: a thin silver-coated quartz wire stretched between the poles of a magnet. As electric current flowed through, the wire was moved. The motion was magnified and then projected onto moving photographic film. The extreme sensitivity of the device allowed it to detect the tiny cardiac currents very accurately.

Einthoven called his machine the electrocardiograph and the recorded electrical impulses an electrocardiogram or EEC. He showed where to position the electrodes and described the regular heart waves and how to interpret electrocardiograms. Through clinical studies, Einthoven identified a number of heart problems with his galvanometer. The English physician Sir Thomas Lewis (1881-1945) established the electrocardiogram as a standard clinical tool.

With refinements in instrumentation and technique, electrocardiography became one of the most useful diagnostic tools in medicine. It is highly accurate, easy to interpret, relatively inexpensive, and permits diagnosis of heart conditions without needle or incision. Furthermore, it pointed the way to similar diagnosis of brain currents through an instrument called an EEG or electroencephalograph.

⁎⁎ Electroencephalogram (EEG)

An electroencephalogram (EEG) is a graphic picture of the electrical activity of the brain. It is made when electrodes on the patient's scalp are connected via wires to a machine known as an electroencephalograph. The

An electro-encephalogram (EEG) recording of a seizure beginning. The electro-encephalograph records the patterns of brain waves and traces them on a sheet of paper.

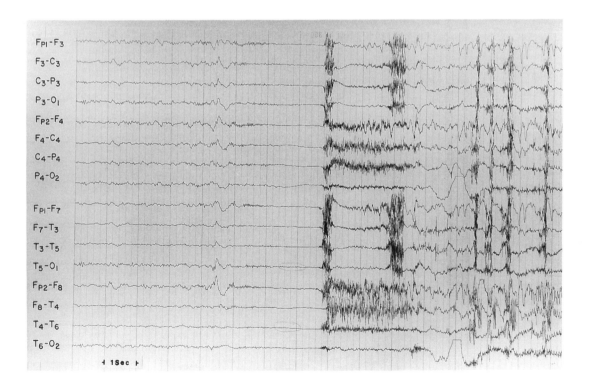

electroencephalograph records the patterns of brain waves and traces them on a sheet of paper.

EEGs are useful in diagnosing neurological conditions that are characterized by distinctive, abnormal patterns of brain waves. These conditions include epilepsy, brain tumors, and strokes. EEGs are also used in investigating psychiatric (mind and behavior) disorders, such as schizophrenia. EEGs also help in defining brain death, a diagnosis that is necessary before the donation of organs for surgical transplants.

Mapping the Brain Waves

A system known as BEAM (brain electrical activity mapping) uses computer technology to combine the signals from the individual electrodes into an overall, color-coded map of the brain's electrical activity.

BEAM can store large amounts of EEG data, compare healthy profiles with abnormal ones, and help diagnose conditions such as dyslexia and schizophrenia, which are usually difficult to detect.

Efforts are underway to use BEAM in matching EEG patterns to specific brain functions. For example, research scientists have used BEAM to map the electrical activity involved in the movement of a monkey's arm. Their studies have shown that when the monkey anticipates moving its arm, the pattern of electrical activity in its brain changes. If efforts such as these are successful, it may one day be possible to use computers and the electrical activity of the brain not only to control artificial limbs but in many other revolutionary applications as well.

It may one day be possible to connect computers to the electrical activity of the brain to control artificial limbs.

⋆⋆ Electrolysis

The smooth metallic finish of older car bumpers was done with electroplating, a type of electrolysis.

Electrolysis is the use of an electric current to break up a compound by causing a chemical reaction. A compound is a mixture of two or more elements. The compound must be in a fluid state, either dissolved or molten, to permit the flow of electricity. Electrolysis is a type of electrochemistry.

One of the first large-scale industrial uses of electrochemistry was the electrolysis of sodium chloride (salt). The electrolytic process is essential for the production of pure metals, reducing the cost considerably. Electrolysis is used to refine aluminum and purify copper. It has even been suggested that the process could provide an environmentally safe source of energy. Sunlight would electrolyze water, and the **hydro-**

gen it produced would be used for fuel in homes, industry, and automobiles. Storage is a big problem, however, and slows the introduction of such technology.

⋆⁺⋆ Electromagnetic wave

Electromagnetic waves are forms of energy that manifest themselves as the phenomena of electricity and magnetism. Electricity and magnetism exist as separate things only in our minds. In nature they occur together. Radio waves and light waves are the most familiar form of electromagnetic waves, but **microwaves**, infrared rays, heat, ultraviolet rays, **X-rays**, and **gamma rays** are all part of the electromagnetic spectrum.

Microwaves, radio waves, light, and X-rays are all types of electromagnetic waves.

Electromagnetic waves are produced by a continuously vibrating electric charge. This process occurs in nature and can be duplicated by people. The number of vibrations per second is called the frequency and is measured in Hertz (cycles per second). The lowest long wave radio frequencies are about 150 kiloHertz. Light has a much higher frequency, at 600,000 GigaHertz. X-rays top out at three billion GigaHertz.

The wavelength is the distance between the successive crests of the wave. The longest radio waves are greater than 6 miles (10 km) in length. In contrast, gamma rays are less than 0.001 nanometers (nm), smaller than an atom. The velocity (speed) of all light waves is equal to the frequency times the wavelength.

Radio waves are electromagnetic waves longer than one millimeter and are subdivided into very high frequency (VHF) and ultra-high frequency (UHF). Very low frequency (VLF) radio waves have wavelengths longer than 6 miles (10 km) with frequencies lower than 30,000 Hertz.

Infrared waves are located between radio waves and visible light. Radio waves that are shorter than one meter are called microwaves, but they share some properties with infrared wavelengths. Infrared radiation is heat, whereas microwaves are generated electronically.

Visible light ranges from 390 nanometers (nm) to 750 nm. Different wavelengths are perceived as different colors by the eye, ranging from red at 680 nm through violet at 400 nm. Wavelengths longer than 750 nm are infrared. Wavelengths shorter than 390 are ultraviolet.

[*]Electromagnetism

The study of electromagnetism led to the creation of the first artificially produced electricity. The story begins more than 2,000 years ago with the ancient Greek philosopher Thales (624-546 B.C.). He discovered that when amber (*elektron* in Greek) was rubbed, it was able to pick up lightweight objects. Lodestone found in the region of Magnesia in western Turkey could also attract **iron**, but without being rubbed. The connection between the attractive abilities of the two materials did not occur to the ancients.

During the eleventh century, the Chinese learned that a freely suspended magnetized needle had the ability to point almost due north. Chinese sailors used it as a compass to show direction. Like the Greeks, they did not make a basic connection: that the cause of the phenomenon was **Earth's magnetic field**.

When a doorbell is pushed, an electric current is tripped, sending a signal to an electromagnet. The magnet attracts the clapper, which hits the bell to create the "ding-dong" chime.

A patient undergoing magnetic resonance imaging (MRI). The principles of electromagnetism have made possible the medical diagnostic technique of MRI, the telegraph, X-rays, and superconductors used to study atoms and electricity.

William Gilbert (1544-1603), experimenting with a freely suspended magnetized needle, discovered that it not only aligned with north and south, but tended to dip down toward the earth. This phenomenon is known as magnetic dip. Gilbert believed that the earth, itself a huge spherical (ball-shaped) magnet, was the source of magnetic influence.

Link Made Between Electrical and Magnetic Charges

The first time magnetism and electricity were linked was in the work of Otto von Guericke. During the 1660s, he built a device that could charge objects with static electricity by rubbing them.

The American diplomat and inventor Benjamin Franklin (1706-1790) discovered "positive" and "negative" electricity. In his famous experiment, he flew a kite during a storm and discovered that lightning was electrical in nature. He saved his own life by using a conductor to channel electricity harmlessly into the ground (a fatal mistake for later scientists trying to duplicate his feat!).

Biological Link

In 1771 Italian anatomist Luigi Galvani discovered that he could make a frog's leg muscle twitch by touching it with probes made of two different metals. He called what he saw "animal electricity." In fact, he had discovered something entirely different, the credit for which would go to another Italian scientist.

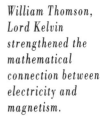

William Thomson, Lord Kelvin strengthened the mathematical connection between electricity and magnetism.

Alessandro Volta (1745-1827) did not believe Galvani's concept of "animal electricity" and set about to disprove the theory. He discovered that the electricity was the result of the interaction between the two different metals of the probes. In 1800 he used that knowledge to invent the first **battery,** the Voltaic pile, which produced continuous electric current. Both Galvani and Volta were immortalized in scientific language. Galvanizing is a process for coating metal while a volt is a standard for measuring electricity.

The next big breakthrough was made by the English physicist Michael Faraday (1791-1867). He discovered that electric energy could be turned into mechanical energy or movement by using magnetism. He found that the reverse is true, that mechanical energy can be used to create electricity. His work laid the foundation for the electric motor.

French mathematician and physicist André Ampère (1775-1836) defined the laws that linked electric current with magnetic force. He described electrostatics as the study of static electricity and electrodynamics as electricity in motion. Today his name, Ampere, is a unit of electric current.

Other scientists were also defining laws of electricity. One was Georg Ohm (1787-1854), who defined the relationship between resistance, electric potential (EMF), and the amount of electrical current that flowed. Today an ohm is defined as a unit of resistance.

Lord Kelvin (born William Thomson; 1824-1907) strengthened the mathematical connection between electricity and magnetism. He developed a theory about oscillating (repeating) currents, which were later used to produce radio waves. Today the Kelvin scale measures temperature.

The final link between electricity and magnetism was forged by Scottish physicist James Clerk Maxwell, working from 1864 to 1873. His mathematical laws unified electric and magnetic phenomena and showed that electricity and magnetism could not exist without each other. He also predicted the existence of electromagnetic waves far beyond those of visible light.

Maxwell's theory was borne out by Heinrich Hertz (1857-1894) in 1881 when he produced "Hertzian waves," dubbed "radio waves." Electromagnetic wavelengths discovered later also obeyed Maxwell's laws. Today Hertz is a unit of frequency.

In 1929 American physicist Robert Van de Graaff (1901-1967) built an electrostatic generator that could create a very high electrical potential and an **electron** stream, used to create X-rays for the treatment of deep tumors.

The principles of electromagnetism have made possible the telegraph, X-rays, magnetic resonance imaging (MRI, a medical diagnostic technique), and superconductors used to study atoms and electricity.

⋆⋆ Electron

Electricity is energy. It occurs when there is an imbalance of **protons** and electrons within atoms. The search to create electricity artificially has been the search to create this imbalance.

In the early 1830s, Michael Faraday was the first to believe that electricity might consist of "atoms of charge." In 1891 the name "electron"
was given to these units of electricity.

The electron is a basic elementary particle involved in a wide variety
of phenomena including not only familiar electrical events, but also the
photoelectric effect, thermionic emission (incandescent light), and, sometimes, **radioactivity**.

By the mid-1920s, a number of physicists began to apply wave and
quantum theory to the electron. At about the same time, theoretical calculations by British physicist Paul Dirac suggested that electrons should

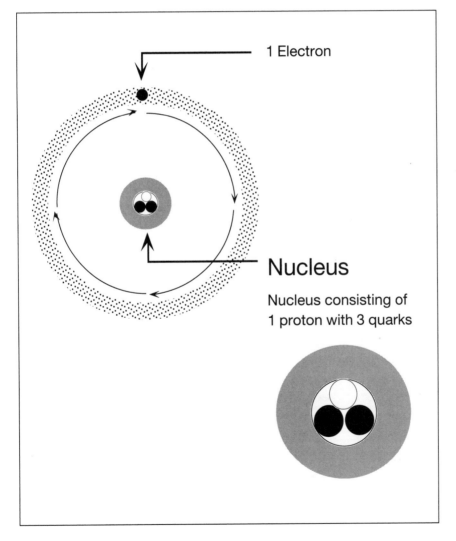

A hydrogen atom.
The electron is one
of a handful of
fundamental
particles that
cannot be broken
down into anything
simpler and that
have no structure.

possess an intrinsic property known as "spin." Dirac's theoretical calculations also suggested the existence of an antiparticle to the electron, a particle identical to the electron in every way except for its charge. That particle, named the "positron," was discovered in 1932 by Carl David Anderson during his study of cosmic rays.

Today, the electron is regarded as one of the handful of fundamental particles, particles that cannot be broken down into anything simpler and that have no structure.

⋆⋆ Elements 104-109

Scientists continue their search for new chemical elements. An element is a type of matter made up of only one kind of atom. At this point, an element has been identified or synthesized at each position in the periodic table through element 108. A great deal of research has already been done on elements 104-109. (In theory we know that 109 exists but it has not yet been isolated.) Controversy surrounds some of the results that have been reported and final decisions on the names and symbols for these elements have yet to be made.

Element 104 is of interest to chemists because it is the first transactinide element. That is, it is the first element to begin a new rare-earth-type row in the periodic table. It occupies the space below hafnium in the table.

In 1964 researchers at the Joint Nuclear Research Institute in Dubno, Ukraine (at the time in the Soviet Union) reported that they had produced

Elements 104-109. The very short half-lives and small quantities of these elements produced so far make the study of their physical and chemical properties very difficult.

PERIODIC TABLE OF ELEMENTS 104-109

104	105	106	107	108	109
Rf	Ha				
257	260	263	262		

an **isotope** of element 104 and proposed naming it kurchatovium (Ku) in honor of the Soviet nuclear physicist Igor Kurchatov (1903-1960). Five years later a team of scientists at the University of California at Berkeley also reported the production of element 104 and suggested the name rutherfordium (Rf) in honor of the British physicist Ernest Rutherford (1871-1937). No decision has yet been made on either of these claims.

The problem of naming the transactinide elements has been addressed by the International Union of Pure and Applied Chemistry (IUPAC). This organization recommends naming these elements with Latin terms for 104, 105, 106, etc., until claims of discovery have been verified. Thus, the IUPAC refers to number 104 as unnilquadium (Unq), number 105 as unnilpentium (Unp), and number 106 as unnilhexium (Unh).

The very short half-lives and small quantities of these elements (called transactinide isotopes) produced so far make the study of their physical and chemical properties very difficult.

See also **Periodic law**

⋆⁺ Elevator

The elevator is a car or platform that moves passengers and freight up and down between the floors of a building. The car, enclosed in a steel frame, glides quickly and smoothly between steel rails inside a vertical shaft. Although the earliest elevators were frustratingly slow and dangerous, today's electric elevators can transport passengers at speeds up to 1,800 feet (550 m) per minute. The elevator has had a tremendous impact on our modern urban landscape: it made the **skyscraper** practical.

Solving the Safety Problem

Freight elevators powered by steam or hydraulic systems were in common use in England and the United States by the early 1800s. Both types had serious drawbacks. The hydraulic elevators were very slow, and passengers wisely refused to ride in the steam elevators—the ropes used to lift their cabs quite often broke, plunging the cab and its contents to the building's basement.

The passenger safety problem, which had slowed elevator use and development, was solved in 1852 by Elisha Graves Otis. As a master mechanic for a New York bedstead factory, Otis invented a safety device

Modern elevator cars are equipped with fire and security alarms, as well as escape hatches in the ceiling.

for his employer's freight elevators. If the rope broke, teeth along the sides of the cab sprang out and clamped onto the elevator's guide rails, which held the cab securely in place.

Modern Developments

The first passenger elevator was installed in the five-story Haughwout department store in New York City in 1857. Hotel and office installations soon followed, and public acceptance of elevator safety grew. City buildings, previously limited to five stories (the extent of most people's stair-climbing ability), suddenly grew to 10 or 12 stories. Structural steel had made the building of skyscrapers technically possible, but elevator safety made such buildings physically and economically feasible.

The elevator has had a tremendous impact on our modern urban landscape: it made the skyscraper practical.

Improved versions of Otis's steam-powered elevator soon followed. An early electric Otis elevator installation in 1889 carried delighted visitors up the newly erected 984-foot Eiffel Tower in Paris. Push-button controls appeared in 1894. The basic modern gearless-traction elevator system was introduced about 1903. After this, efforts to improve the elevator focused on convenience and efficiency features such as automatic leveling, power control of doors, automatic operation, and increased speed.

Most of today's elevators are powered by electric traction systems, with an electric motor turning the sheave (pulley) around which the hoisting cables run. No doubt Elisha Otis, whose factory only employed eight or ten men at the time of his death in 1861, would be astonished to know that more than two million elevators are now in service around the world.

⋆⋆ Endorphin and enkephalin

When a person is injured, pain impulses travel up the spinal cord to the brain, which then releases endorphins and enkephalins, the body's natural painkillers. Enkephalins block pain signals in the spinal cord, while endorphins are thought to block pain principally at the brain stem. Both are **morphine**-like substances whose functions are similar to those of opiate (based upon opium) drugs.

Today, the word "endorphin" is used generically to describe both groups of painkillers. These naturally occurring opiates include enkephalins (methionine and leucine), endorphins (alpha, beta, gamma, and delta) and a growing number of synthetic (artificial) compounds.

Natural and Artificial Painkillers

In the mid-1960s, some scientists proposed theories that said the opiate narcotics (opium, heroin, morphine) mimic the actions of naturally occurring chemicals within the brain and act as painkillers by manipulating the brain's receivers for those naturally occurring substances.

Brain chemistry investigations were speeded by the discovery in the late 1970s that there are specific sites in the brain to which opiate drugs attach themselves and perform their functions.

Researchers subsequently identified the two naturally occurring chemicals—endorphins and enkephalins—as producing morphine-like effects. This offered opportunities for developing drugs similar in structure to the natural pain-killing substances. The power of mind-producing pain killers and their psychological effects on the body were revealed in 1978.

⋆⋆ Endoscope

Sometimes called the fiberscope, the endoscope is an instrument that allows doctors to view the inner workings of the human body without having to perform surgery. Endoscopes are primarily used in the health care field, but they can be used for industrial purposes, examining such hard-to-reach places as the inside of fuel tanks and nuclear reactors.

The endoscope is a flexible narrow tube containing several bundles of hair-thin glass fibers that are covered with a reflective coating. A highly intense light source, usually a **halogen lamp**, is used to transmit light along one bundle of fibers toward the target area. Another bundle of fibers carries an image of the target area back up the tube where it is viewed through an eyepiece.

Endoscopes allow doctors to see the inside of a patient's brain, bones, and arteries.

Medical Uses

The modern endoscope can perform an amazing variety of medical procedures. In addition to the **fiber optic** bundles that transmit light, the endoscopic tube also contains air and water channels for flushing water through or inflating targeted areas.

Tiny forceps (tweezers) can be placed at the tip of the endoscope to take specimen samples for laboratory analysis and to perform simple operations such as removing colon polyps or gallstones. Endoscopes can also be used to stop hemorrhaging (heavy bleeding) by delivering **laser** beams directly to the point of bleeding. The **blood** thickens and the bleeding is stopped.

Different types of endoscopes are specially designed to examine specific parts of the body:

- Angioscopes pass through the arteries that carry blood to the heart.
- Arthroscopes explore the interiors of joints.
- Bronchoscopes are used with a special dye and fluorescent light to detect lung malignancies (cancers).
- Gastroscopes probe the stomach and upper intestinal tract.
- Laparoscopes diagnose and treat abdominal conditions.

Opposite page: A Porsche automobile engine. The introduction of engines in the early eighteenth century would change society forever.

✦ Engine

An engine is a machine that changes or converts heat into mechanical power. Engines are complex tools that have been developed to make life easier. Like all tools, engines need a source of energy.

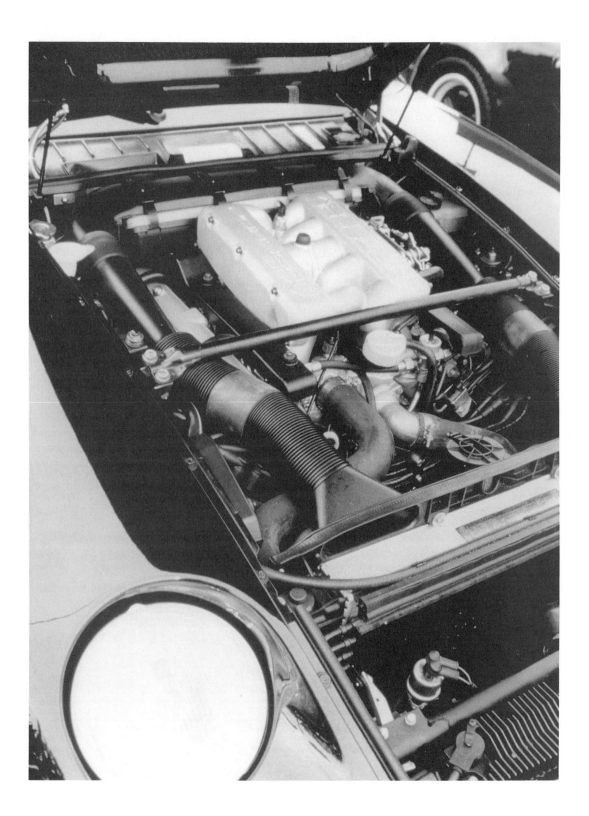

Industrial Revolution

Before the Industrial Revolution, which began in England about 1760, products were made by hand. Cloth, rugs, iron, furniture, and dishes were all made by craftspeople working alone or in small groups.

But early in the 1700s, several inventors struggled to build machines that would do the simple, repetitive tasks done by hand. These inventors first turned to waterfalls, and used the energy of the falling water as fuel for the engines that drove their weaving and smelting machines. Next, inventors used steam as a fuel source. By burning coal, they could boil water and use its steam to drive the engines.

The Industrial Revolution changed British society forever. As England entered the Modern Age, so did the rest of Europe and then the United States. Huge machines and engines in factories now made almost all of the products people used. The factories drew people from the countryside, creating a huge new working class, one that was often underpaid and overworked.

But man's love affair with engines was just starting. In later years he would turn from steam to oil to power his engines. Next he would try diesel and gasoline to fuel his transportation inventions. Ultimately, rocket engines would prove strong enough to break through the hold of Earth's gravity and send man into space.

See also **Engine oil; Internal combustion engine; Jet engine; Steam engine**

⋆⋆ Engine oil

The first **internal combustion engine** was developed in 1680 by the Dutch physicist Christiaan Huygens, who experimented with gunpowder as a fuel. The engine was far too dangerous to be practical, but the idea of an internal combustion engine continued to fascinate inventors.

Later inventors employed coal gas, which was widely used to light city streets. Frenchman Jean-Joseph Étienne Lenoir is usually credited with developing in 1859 the world's first practical internal combustion engine, which was fueled by coal gas.

Also in 1859, Edwin Drake struck oil in Pennsylvania, an event that changed forever how the world generated power. The oil was first refined to yield kerosene, a fuel that immediately began to replace coal gas as the fuel of choice for internal combustion engines.

Many innovators altered their engines to burn the gasoline made possible by Drake's discovery. The most notable of these innovators was the German Rudolf Diesel, who saw fuel oil as a cheaper and more desirable fuel.

Diesel's goal was to develop an engine that would convert the greatest amount of a fuel's energy to usable power. **Steam engines**, for example, convert about 7 percent of the energy contained in the burnt fuel into mechanical energy. Diesel was convinced that he could design an engine that would capture more than 70 percent of the fuel's energy.

His theory, based on thermodynamics (the study of heat and energy), led to an engine with a radically improved performance. Diesel received a patent on his engine in 1892.

Pros and Cons of Diesel Engines

On the plus side, the diesel engine eliminated the ignition system and

The diesel engine can also be found in trucks, buses, tractors, and other agricultural machinery. Diesels burn crude fuels while delivering an efficient amount of the fuel's energy as usable power.

carburetor, two complicated mechanical systems. Plus, diesel fuel is cheaper than gasoline and, because it is less volatile, it is a safer fuel to use.

On the negative side, diesel engines weigh considerably more than a gasoline engine that produces the same amount of usable power. This weight cuts into their fuel efficiency. Diesel engines also run roughly at low speeds, they have high levels of pollutants in their exhaust, and the exhaust odor smells worse than that emitted by conventional gasoline engines.

Despite these disadvantages, the diesel engine's efficiency has led to its widespread use, and the engine has undergone several refinements since the death of Rudolf Diesel in 1913. It was first installed in a ship in 1910, and in an **automobile** in 1922. The diesel-electric locomotive has all but replaced the steam engine for rail power. The diesel engine can also be found in trucks, buses, tractors, and other agricultural machinery. It is almost the only choice for industrial power throughout the world because of its ability to burn crude fuels while delivering an efficient amount of the fuel's energy as usable power.

See also **Oil refining**

⋆ Enzyme

Since ancient times, people have observed enzymes at work fermenting wine and beer, turning sour milk into cheese, and causing bread dough to rise.

Enzymes are complex proteins that act as catalysts or stimulators for the countless biochemical reactions that keep humans, animals, plants, and microorganisms alive. Enzymes occur in every living **cell**. They have relatively large molecules that contain one or more **amino acid** chains. The sequence of amino acids within the chains and the distinctive way each chain folds into its own characteristic three-dimensional shape help determine the enzyme's particular activity.

In the Body

The typical animal cell (roughly one-billionth the size of a drop of water) contains about 3,000 different enzymes, almost all programmed to perform specific chemical reactions necessary for **metabolism** (production of energy).

For example, in the digestive tract certain enzymes are involved in breaking down oversized **fat**, carbohydrate, and protein molecules into smaller and easier-to-absorb molecules. A different set of enzymes assists in moving these molecules into the bloodstream. Other enzymes then use some of these molecules in the biosynthesis of new cellular structures.

Serious problems can result when a particular enzyme is actually missing. In a number of hereditary human diseases—such as **phenylketonuria (PKU)** and galactosemia—geneticists have discovered that the affected individuals are born missing certain specific enzymes. Some of these enzyme-deficiency diseases can now be effectively treated and many researchers are concentrating on the search for more of these disorders, which may ultimately revolutionize the practice of medicine.

Industrial Uses

Enzymes have important industrial and commercial uses as well. Since ancient times, people have observed enzymes at work fermenting wine and beer, turning sour milk into cheese, and causing bread dough to rise. However, these reactions were generally considered as **fermentations** of some mysterious kind and only vaguely understood. Then, in the early 1800s, biochemists began taking a closer look at the "ferments" causing some of these reactions. They discovered diastase, the first enzyme to be isolated and prepared in concentrated form.

Since then thousands of enzymes have been discovered. They are used to help get clothes clean, clear fat out of plugged drains, and make fruit juice clear.

See also **Blood clot dissolving agent; Digestion; Fermentation; Restriction enzyme**

⋆⋆ Epinephrine (adrenaline)

Epinephrine (ep-i-nef-rin), also known as adrenaline, was the first **hormone** to be discovered. It is produced constantly in small amounts by the adrenal glands, which are endocrine glands located on the kidneys.

When we face anxiety, danger, or other stress, our brain sends a chemical message to the adrenal glands, which respond by increasing epinephrine production. This elevated epinephrine level in turn increases our alertness, energy level, heart rate, blood pressure, and strength. This body state is known as "fight or flight." Your physical strength increases, making you able to combat the problem at hand ("fight") or escape the situation quickly ("flight").

In the early 1900s epinephrine was available for medical purposes such as reviving persons suffering from hemorrhage (excessive bleeding) and shock. However, it was not until 1905 that the British physiologist

Epinephrine helps the person in trouble by giving him or her extra strength to fight or escape.

William Bayliss and Ernest Starling introduced the concept of a hormone—a substance that is produced by one organ and carried by the blood to another organ, where it influences its functions. Only then did scientists realize that epinephrine was a hormone.

The significance of epinephrine and other hormones in the body's operations was discovered by the American physiologist Walter Bradford Cannon (1871-1945), after he worked with injured World War I (1914-18) soldiers. Cannon was born in Prairie du Chien, Wisconsin, and earned a medical degree at Harvard University.

Other scientists had already studied the body as an internal environment and the interrelation of **metabolism**, hormones, and the **immune system**. In 1926 Cannon developed the concept of homeostasis, an organism's ability to remain stable internally, even when the surrounding environment exerts great stress upon it, such as hunger, thirst, and sudden danger. Epinephrine helps the human body maintain homeostasis.

⋆⋆ Eraser

The first erasers for wiping out lead pencil marks were pieces of bread. The modern eraser made of rubber appeared in the eighteenth century. A vegetable gum from South America called *caoutchouc* was an early material used in erasers. When the English scientist Joseph Priestley (1733-1804) noted that he could use *caoutchouc* to rub out lead pencil marks in a manuscript, *caoutchouc* got its familiar name of "rubber."

The idea for attaching a rubber eraser to the end of a pencil was patented in 1858 by both Hyman Lipman of Philadelphia, Pennsylvania, and Joseph Rechendorfer of New York City. The eraser with a hollowed-out end into which a pencil could be inserted was invented by J. B. Blair of Philadelphia in 1867.

Modern erasers are a mixture of rubber, vegetable oil, sulfur, and pumice. **Plastic** and synthetic rubber are also used to produce erasers.

⋆⋆ Ethylene

Just about every home and business in the modern world contains products made with ethylene. This organic gas is the starting point for the manu-

Plant Growth

During the twentieth century, scientists discovered that ethylene causes fruit to ripen more quickly by functioning as a growth regulator. In the late 1800s, although people knew that gas lighting could stimulate growth in plants, they did not realize that the effect was due to ethylene's presence in the fumes and smoke given off by the lights.

facture of most **plastic** materials. These plastics show up in containers for soft drinks and mouthwash, coverings for electric wires, and plastic bowls and wrapping for saving food.

About half of the ethylene produced in the United States goes to make **polyethylene**, the most important derivative (offshoot) of ethylene. Synthetic (artificial) rubber is also made with an ethylene derivative, and one of ethylene's compounds is used to make antifreeze for car radiators.

Ethylene belongs to the family of **hydrocarbons** called olefins. Most ethylene is produced by heating ethane and propane. Oil refineries also generate some ethylene as a by-product. Today, ethylene gas is used to regulate plant growth in greenhouses, and ethylene is sprayed on some crops before or after harvesting to speed ripening.

Charles Darwin began to explain evolution as we understand it today.

⋆⃰ Evolutionary theory

Today, the industrialized nations have come to regard evolution theory as historical fact, seeing fossils as proof that species evolved gradually. However, the concept of evolution only emerged in the early nineteenth century. Up until that time, the Western world had generally regarded as fact the Adam and Eve account of creation provided in the Biblical book of Genesis. The Genesis account held that the world had been created relatively recently, that every species was created separately and distinctly, and that these species had remained unchanged over the centuries.

*As the
eighteenth-
century
scientific
community
began
attempting to
classify plants
and animals
systematically,
the immense
diversity and
inter-
relatedness of
living things
made scientists
doubt the
traditional
view of
creation.*

What caused people to suddenly question the scientific probability of the Genesis version? As the eighteenth-century scientific community began attempting to classify plants and animals systematically, the immense diversity and interrelatedness of living things made scientists doubt the traditional view. The plant and animal fossils found by excavators were particularly at issue. These fossils implied not only that the history of Earth extended back much further than previously believed, but that life developed only gradually and unevenly from simple to advanced organisms.

In 1809 the French botanist Jean Baptiste de Lamarck (1744-1829) made an important attempt to explain this complexity of organic (plant and animal) life. Although he did not use the term "evolution," Lamarck argued that species gradually progressed over time from simpler to more complex types. To account for this change, Lamarck proposed that organisms possess both an innate (inborn) drive toward perfection and an ability to adapt to their environment.

Lamarck further believed that acquired characteristics could be passed on from generation to generation. For example, Lamarck reasoned that the ancestors of the giraffe, in reaching for high leaves to eat, would have stretched and elongated their necks. This trait, he believed, was then passed on to their descendants. Although this belief in the transmission of acquired traits has since been proven wrong, Lamarck was correct in assuming that traits could somehow be inherited and that, in theory, this process could lead, over long periods to significant evolutionary changes.

Darwin's Key Ideas

It was the English naturalist Charles Darwin (1809-1882) who began to explain evolution (in Darwin's term, "descent with modification") as we understand it today. Darwin's theories were based on the earth and plant and animal studies he did in the 1830s during travels in South America and South Sea (Pacific) Islands. Darwin's detailed observations provided a considerable body of evidence for evolutionary change. He then theorized that the fossils indicated that some species had become extinct, although species that appeared related to them had survived.

Darwin also recognized that similar but not identical species were found in different geographical regions. In the Galapagos Islands, furthermore, Darwin observed that the beaks of different types of finch birds were evidently adapted to the food supplies of the geographically distinct islands they populated. Similar adaptations characterized the local species of giant tortoises.

In *On the Origin of Species* in 1859, Darwin proposed that species mutate and diverge and that they are not fixed in form. Darwin's evidence suggested that many species had common ancestors. Thus, lizards and rabbits are similar in their embryonic stage, and the bones in human arms and legs correspond to those in the limbs of dogs or horses. To explain these parallels, Darwin proposed that species had branched and evolved through natural selection.

Natural selection implies that, given the competition for limited resources such as food, those organisms best adapted to their specific environment are most likely to survive, reproduce, and transmit traits to their offspring. This process, occurring in the midst of environmental changes, causes the helpful traits of members of a particular species to predominate and the unhelpful traits to be lost. Over thousands of years, certain forms of life accumulate enough changes for an apparently new and distinct species to emerge. Thus while horses and hippopotamuses have common ancestors, each today is a separate species.

Darwin's theories, though bold and controversial, took place within the context of a dynamic nineteenth-century scientific and intellectual community. Thus, Darwin's *On the Origin of Species* was modeled on Charles Lyell's (1797-1875) similarly groundbreaking *Principles of Geology,* published in the 1830s. Alfred Russell Wallace (1823-1913), doing his own independent studies in the East Indies, formulated his own theory of natural evolution at the same time as Darwin.

It was English philosopher Herbert Spencer (1820-1903) who coined the phrase "the survival of the fittest." This phrase does not mean that the strongest species will necessarily flourish, but rather that those species best "fitted" to their environments have the best chances of survival. Other prominent intellectuals were vital in the process of debating, elaborating, and circulating Darwin's theories.

It was the presence of this community that allowed Darwin to publish his second important book, *The Descent of Man,* in 1871. This publication, which exposed Darwin to considerable religious opposition and public scorn, followed through on his earlier work. In this book, Darwin asserted that human beings had descended from, and were biologically related to, earlier life forms.

Even as the scientific community came to accept Darwin's theories of "descent with modification" and evolution through natural selection, they recognized that Darwin had failed to adequately explain how biological variations were produced or passed on.

Natural selection implies that, given the competition for limited resources such as food, those organisms best adapted to their specific environment are most likely to survive, reproduce, and transmit traits to their offspring.

Mendel Introduces Heredity's Role

This issue was essentially resolved by the Austrian monk and botanist Gregor Mendel. In the 1860s he tried to isolate the basic unit of **heredity** now known as the **gene**. Working in the garden of the monastery, Mendel discovered differences among varieties of common garden peas (such as variations in shape, size, flowering, coloring, and seed characteristics) and believed they were due to paired units of heredity. Mendel was the first to consider that these molecular "blueprints," passed on from parents to offspring, determined which features a living organism will inherit.

Gregor Mendel was the first to consider that genes, passed on from parents to offspring, determined which features a living organism will inherit.

The integration of Darwin's "descent with modification" and Mendel's work in genetics was substantially achieved by the Russian-American Theodosius Dobzhansky, who published his influential book *Genetics and the Origin of Species* in 1937. Dobzhansky's experiments with fruit flies clarified the process of evolutionary adaptation by demonstrating the variability of genes and thus the possibility of rapid evolutionary change through genetic mutation and change.

"Neo-Darwinism," as the blend of Darwinism and Mendelism genetics is often called, thus recognizes that evolution involves not only physical and behavioral traits, but also the genes that serve as the basis for those traits. This process of genetic evolution is known as "genetic drift."

Continuous and substantial changes have been made in the study of evolution in the twentieth century. Most recent evolutionary theory suggests the possibility of periods of rapid change, as well as periods of long-term change.

On the heredity research front, scientists have been equally active. Walter S. Sutton, Theodor Boveri, Wilhelm Johannsen, Thomas Hunt Morgan, and Hermann Muller have investigated the complex relationship among chromosomes, genes, and the laws of heredity. Biometricians (those who study biological phenomena) such as Ronald Fisher, John Haldane, and Reginald Crundall Punnet have used mathematical and statistical techniques to analyze genetic changes, thereby establishing the field of population genetics.

Biologist Julian Huxley made important contributions to the field of embryology and other areas. The paleontologist George Simpson focused on the intercontinental migration patterns of ancient species. And James Watson and Francis Crick introduced a model for **deoxyribonucleic acid** (**DNA**) to explain the chemical basis of genes, heredity, and evolution. The ongoing human genome project is science's attempt to map out the human gene pattern.

See also **Chromosome; DNA (deoxyribonucleic acid)**

⁺₊* Expert system

An expert system is a computer program that combines a knowledge base of information about a particular field with a system of rules that applies the knowledge to specific situations. Such a system can analyze a problem in a given discipline and provide solutions for it. An expert system is considered a form of **artificial intelligence**.

Expert systems analyze huge amounts of information so people can make better, faster decisions.

Medical Diagnoses

One expert system called MYCIN diagnoses blood-related infections. The computer program analyzes data input by the physician, asks relevant questions about the patient's test results and condition, and then uses this information to provide a diagnosis and recommendations for treatment.

Although MYCIN's accuracy seems to be quite good, many physicians are still unwilling to rely on a computer to diagnose serious illness. A training program based on MYCIN called GUIDON is, however, being used in medical school classrooms.

Another medical expert system, PUFF, has found more use in real-life situations. When a patient undergoes lung tests, PUFF receives the data from the tests as they are carried out. Like MYCIN, PUFF provides the physician with a diagnosis and suggested treatment.

Uses in Business

Expert systems have become very useful in the field of finance and accounting as well. For example, an expert system called TAXMAN has been developed to help the many people bewildered by their annual tax returns. TAXMAN operates on a personal computer (PC) and creates a return by prompting the user to input data, performing necessary calculations, and neatly printing the results.

A host of other expert systems has been devised, including programs to perform geological studies of land sites; determine the cause of diesel locomotive malfunctions; solve difficult mathematical equations; help sales people select merchandise for customers; and aid computer programmers in designing and "debugging" other computer systems.

See also **Computer, digital; Microcomputer**

⁎⋆ *Explorer 1*

On October 4, 1957, the former Soviet Union launched the first **satellite** to break through the atmosphere and orbit the Earth. The space vessel was called *Sputnik 1*. Thus began the great "Space Race" of the 1960s between the Soviet Union and the United States. The American government tried to play down the event, but began to aggressively pursue their own satellite program.

Vanguard Fails

The German-born American scientist Wernher von Braun had developed a Jupiter-C **rocket** for the U.S. Army and asked the government for permission to launch a satellite with it. The government turned him down, however, having already decided on a navy project called Vanguard. On December 6, 1957, officials gathered the press to witness the first launch of the Vanguard rocket. But after hesitating a few feet above the ground, the Vanguard exploded into flames.

After other disasters with Vanguard, von Braun was given the green light. On January 31, 1958, his Jupiter-C rocket lifted off. Two and a half minutes later, the first stage shut down and the next fired. Orbit was attained. The satellite itself orbited with the top stage of the rocket. It ranged in distance from the earth between 218 miles (352 km) and 1,586 miles (2,554 km).

Satellite's Tasks

Explorer 1 was small in comparison to the *Sputniks:* it weighed only 10.5 pounds (4.7 kg). No doubt the Soviets had larger rockets to launch their huge satellites, but the American representative had its advantages.

Unlike *Sputnik 1, Explorer 1* contained more than just instruments to measure the temperature and density of the upper atmosphere. It had a micrometer to measure debris (garbage) in space and a **radiation detector** that found intense rings of radiation surrounding the earth at great heights. Later, these rings were called the **Van Allen radiation belts,** named after the scientist who designed the experiment. *Explorer 1* thus proved the great scientific value of satellites.

See also **Van Allen belts**

⋆⋆ Eye disorders

The eye is the delicate organ of sight that tells us about the natural world around us.

The following are fairly common vision problems that do not threaten vision and can often be corrected with **eyeglasses** or **contact lenses**, or with surgery:

- Hyperopia or farsightedness is a condition in which a person sees faraway objects in sharp focus but cannot clearly see nearby objects. To correct hyperopia, convex corrective lenses are used.

- Myopia or nearsightedness is a problem in which a person cannot clearly see distant objects. Concave lenses can be worn to permit focusing for objects far away. Radial keratotomy is

The human eye and two common eye disorders. Light from an object first strikes the transparent covering of the eyeball, the cornea. The light passes through the lens, a clear, flexible disc, which bends the light rays enough so that they focus on the back of the eye, which is called the retina.

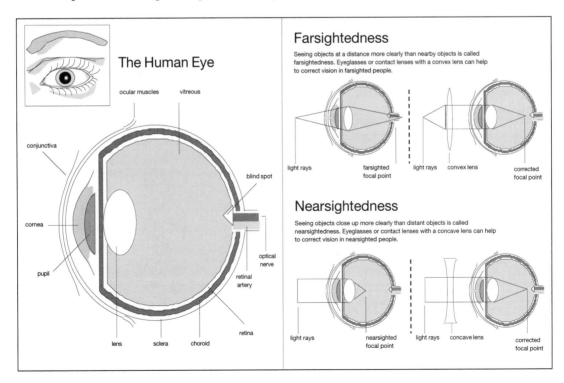

The Human Eye

ocular muscles   vitreous

conjunctiva

blind spot

cornea

optical nerve

pupil

retinal artery

retina

lens   sclera   choroid

Farsightedness

Seeing objects at a distance more clearly than nearby objects is called farsightedness. Eyeglasses or contact lenses with a convex lens can help to correct vision in farsighted people.

light rays   farsighted focal point   light rays   convex lens   corrected focal point

Nearsightedness

Seeing objects close up more clearly than distant objects is called nearsightedness. Eyeglasses or contact lenses with a concave lens can help to correct vision in nearsighted people.

light rays   nearsighted focal point   light rays   concave lens   corrected focal point a surgical procedure that involves making incisions on the cornea to correct myopia. It was first done in Japan in 1955. In the 1990s, follow-up interviews on hundreds of patients who underwent the procedure show that two-thirds of the patients were able to stop wearing corrective eyeglasses or contact lenses. A newer, "corneal sculpting" laser surgery that takes only about 30 seconds to complete may be approved sometime in the near future to correct myopia.

• Astigmatism is an eye condition that makes objects appear blurred. The condition may cause headaches or eye strain. It can be corrected with glasses and certain kinds of contact lenses.

• Presbyopia is a problem in which the eye loses its elasticity and can no longer change focuses quickly from near to far-away objects. The condition is usually associated with age and becomes evident after 40. Usually presbyopia is corrected by wearing reading glasses.

• Strabismus is a condition in which one eye cannot focus with the other. Sometimes in children the condition will self-correct or surgery is recommended to "uncross" the eyes.

Laser surgery is an option for correcting some eye disorders, such as myopia and degenerative retinopathy.

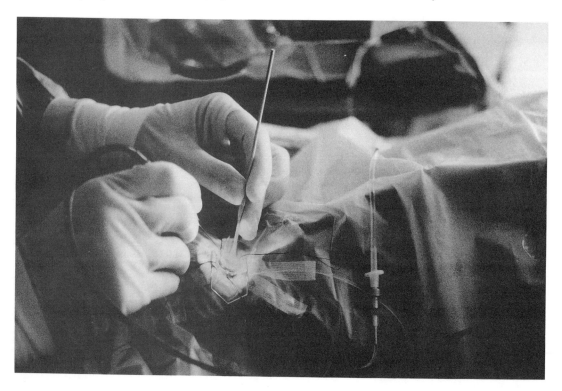

- Color blindness is the inability to distinguish between certain colors, most often red and green. It is a genetic condition that cannot be cured, but contact lenses to correct color blindness have recently been invented by Jay Schlanger.

Blindness is a complete or partial loss of vision. People born with the inability to see have congenital blindness. Other people who lose their vision through accident or disease have acquired blindness. The following are eye disorders, some of which can lead to blindness if untreated:

- **Cataracts** are spots on the lens of the eye that cut off the light that passes through. They are sometimes attributed to age, although they may form in children or persons with diabetes or other conditions. Recent evidence shows that cataracts can be caused by exposure to ultraviolet light (including sunlight). If unchecked, cataracts cause the entire lens to become cloudy and blindness results.

- **Glaucoma** causes the eyeball to harden because fluid inside the eye does not drain properly. This leads to an increase in pressure that can kill the optic nerve and cause blindness.

- Keratitis is an inflammation of the cornea of the eye. In some cases both the cornea and another eye part, the conjunctiva, are inflamed. These two conditions represent a large portion of all eye disease. Keratitis follows cataracts and glaucoma as a leading cause of blindness. The condition has many causes, including injury, infection, radiation, irritation by chemicals, or an allergy.

  With the use of contact lenses, especially soft and extended-wear contacts, physicians are seeing an increase in the number of cases of ulcerative (irritated) keratitis, probably because people wear their lenses around the clock without disinfecting them.

- Conjunctivitis is a fairly common, very contagious inflammation of the eyelid caused by infection and usually treated with drug therapy.

- Trachoma is an extremely infectious eye disease which inflames the lining of the eyelid and forms small ulcers (sores) on the cornea. It is more prevalent in developing countries than in the United States.

- Ophthalmia neonatorum affects the eyes of newborns. Symptoms are ulcers (sores) on the cornea, swelling of eyelids, and

With the use of contact lenses, physicians are seeing an increase in the number of cases of ulcerative (irritated) keratitis, probably because people wear their lenses around the clock without disinfecting them.

pus discharge. It is often caused by **gonorrhea**, a sexually transmitted disease that is passed on from mother to child.

- Retinitis is an inflammation of the retina that may be caused by bacterial infection, injury of the eyeball, or intense light. Degenerative retinopathy may be brought on by many conditions, including advanced age, diabetes, high blood pressure, **arteriosclerosis** (a heart condition), **anemia** (lack of iron), and leukemia (cancer of the blood). Retinopathy is successfully treated with argon laser surgery.

Leonardo da Vinci and Benjamin Franklin were two noted inventors who turned their attention to correcting vision problems.

⁂ Eyeglasses

Eyeglasses are corrective lenses mounted in frames that help people with vision problems to see clearly. People suffer from many different types of vision problems:

- Some people can see distant objects clearly but find nearby objects blurry. They suffer from hyperopia or farsightedness.

- Some people suffer from myopia or nearsightedness, where only nearby objects can be seen clearly.

- Some people suffer from a condition called presbyopia, which is usually associated with age and becomes evident after 40. Presbyopia causes people to be somewhat farsighted. Sometimes this is corrected by wearing bifocals, or eyeglasses with two different lenses. A person with presbyopia can look through the bottom lens while reading and use the top lens for distant objects.

The invention of eyeglasses has a long and colorful history. It is said that during the days of the Roman Empire, the emperor Nero watched exhibitions in the Coliseum holding a jewel with curved facets up to one eye. Roger Bacon, an English scholar, is said to have suggested the use of eyeglasses in the 1200s.

Early eyeglasses had glass lenses mounted on heavy frames of wood, lead, or copper. Natural materials of leather, bone, and horn were later used and then lighter frames of steel were made by the early seventeenth century. Tortoiseshell frames came into use in the eighteenth century. In 1746 a French optician named Thomin invented actual eyeglass frames that could be placed over the ears and nose.

In the United States, statesman and scientist Benjamin Franklin designed the first bifocals in 1760. In this way he could use the top lens to see distant objects and use the bottom lens to read without needing two pair of glasses. The two lenses were joined in a metal frame.

In England in 1827, Sir George Biddle Airy (1801-1892), an English astronomer and mathematician, made the first glasses to correct astigmatism, a condition he himself had. Astigmatism is blurry vision caused by irregular curves in the cornea, the transparent covering of the eye. The irregular curvature makes it impossible for light rays to focus on a single point. To correct this, the exact area of the irregularity of the cornea is located, and a corresponding area on the eyeglass lens is ground to bring light rays passing through that area into proper focus.

Benjamin Franklin designed the first bifocals in 1760 by joining two lenses in a metal frame. The top lens was used to see distant objects and the bottom lens to read.

Eyeglasses Make a Fashion Statement

Today eyeglasses come in many styles and designs. Frames are generally made of metal or **plastic**, and lenses are made of glass or plastic. In 1955 the first unbreakable lenses were made and in 1971 a new lens came out that combined the properties of plastic with glass.

Eyewear has been revolutionized with the invention of the **contact lens,** a tiny corrective lens that is placed directly on the cornea of the eye. Contact lenses were originally made of glass and produced in Europe near the turn of the twentieth century.

In 1936 I. G. Farben, a German company, made the first contact lens from Plexiglas—a plastic still used today for "hard" contact lenses. An American inventor named Tuohy began use of a lens that covers only the cornea and in 1964 a Czech named Wichterle made the first flexible or "soft" lens. Today people wear an array of hard and soft lenses, extended wear lenses, tinted lenses, lenses that can correct astigmatism, and lenses to correct color blindness.

Master Index

A

Abacists *5:* 904
Abacus *2:* 298; *5:* 904
Abbe, Cleveland *6:* 1067, 1148
Abdomen *4:* 662
Abelson, Philip *4:* 730
Abercromby, Ralph *6:* 1149
Abortion *5:* 907
Abplanalp, Robert H. *1:* 19
Abrasive *1:* **1-2**
Absolute scale *1:* 3
Absolute zero *1:* **2-3**
Acetaminophen *3:* 571
Acetic acid *1:* **3-4**, 7; *5:* 845;
    6: 1170
Acetylcholine *1:* **4-6**; *6:* 1040
Acheson, Edward G. *1:* 1
Acid *1:* 3, 9; *4:* 740
Acid and base *1:* 4, **6-9**; *3:*
    563
Acid rain *1:* **9-12**; *4:* 744
Acoustics, physiological *1:*
    12-13
Acquired blindness *2:* 409
Acromegaly *3:* 560
Acropolis *1:* 11
Acrylic plastic *1:* 13-14
Acrylonitrile *3:* 459
ACTH (adrenocorticotropic
    hormone) *1:* **14-15**; *3:* 553
Actinium *5:* 820
Acupuncture *1:* **15-17**
Adams, John Couch *4:* 728;
    5: 845

Adams' New York Gum *2:*
    265
Adams, Thomas, Jr. *2:* 265
Adams, Thomas, Sr. *2:* 265
Addison's disease *3:* 553
Addison, Thomas *3:* 553
Addition *1:* 38; *2:* 227, 274,
    281, 294, 299
Additive three-color process
    2: 278
Ader, Clement *6:* 1019
Adhesives and adhesive tape
    1: **17-19**; *2:* 345; *5:* 853,
    856
Adiabatic demagnetization *2:*
    331
Adipose tissue *3:* 447
Adrenal gland cortex
    hormones *3:* 552
Adrenalin *1:* 5
Advanced X-ray Astrophysics
    Facility (AXAF) *6:* 1005
Advertising *3:* 550
Advil *3:* 572
Aëdes aegypti *6:* 1172
Aero Foam *3:* 462
Aerodynamics *6:* 1157
Aeronautics *6:* 1157
Aerosol spray *1:* 19-20
Agate *3:* 444
Agent Orange *2:* 263
Agricultural crops *2:* 336
Agriculture *3:* 453, 499, 500
AIDS (Acquired Immune
    Deficiency Syndrome) *1:*

20-24; *2:* 246, 263; *3:* 497,
    541, 575; *5:* 848, 893; *6:*
    1134
AIDS therapies and vaccines
    1: **24-26**
Aiken, Howard *2:* 300
Air *2:* 241
Airbag, automobile *1:* **26-27**
Air conditioning *1:* **27-29**
Aircraft *1:* 14, 19, **29-36**, 41,
    46; *2:* 305; *3:* 459, 585,
    594, 535; *4:* 635, 688, 703;
    5: 925, 933, 927; *6:* 1014,
    1019, 1035, 1156
Airplane *4:* 761; *6:* 1000
Air pollution *1:* 9; *3:* 514; *4:*
    774; *5:* 824
Airship *3:* 564
Airy, George Biddle *2:* 411
alaia *6:* 1036
Alchemy *3:* 562; *6:* 1088
Alcohol *2:* 245; *3:* 450, 509;
    6: 1170, 1171
Alcohol, distilling of *1:* **37-38**
Alcoholic hepatitis *3:* 542
Alcoholism *1:* 37
Aldrin, Edwin "Buzz" *4:* 710;
    6: 984
Aleksandrov, Pavel
    Sergeevich *6:* 1076
Alexanderson, Ernst *6:* 1058
Algebra *5:* 884
Algorists *5:* 905
Algorithm *1:* **38**; *2:* 227
Alhazen *4:* 653

Boldfaced numbers indicate main entry pages; italicized numbers indicate volume number

Boldfaced numbers indicate main entry pages; italicized numbers indicate volume number

Boldfaced numbers indicate main entry pages; italicized numbers indicate volume number

Boldfaced numbers indicate main entry pages; italicized numbers indicate volume number

Boldfaced numbers indicate main entry pages; italicized numbers indicate volume number

Boldfaced numbers indicate main entry pages; italicized numbers indicate volume number

H

Haber, Fritz *3:* 456; *4:* 743
Hafnium *2:* 390; *5:* 820
Haggerty, Patrick *2:* 228
Hair care *3:* **519-521**
Hair-care products *2:* 326
Hair dryer *3:* 519
Hair dyes *3:* 520
Hair extensions *3:* 520
Hairpiece *3:* 520
Hair spray *3:* 520
Hair weaving *3:* 521
Haldane, John Burdon *2:* 404; *4:* 722; *5:* 855
Hale, George Ellery *5:* 946; *6:* 1055
Hall, Chester Moor *6:* 1054
Halley, Edmond *4:* 690, 738; *6:* 1148
Hall, Lloyd A. *3:* 476
Hall, Samuel Read *6:* 1045
Hallucinogen *3:* **521-523**
Halogen lamp *2:* 394; *3:* **523-524**
Halol *6:* 1088
Haloperidol *6:* 1088
Halsted, William *2:* 277
Haltran *3:* 572
Hamilton, Alice *4:* 741
Hammond, Laurens *4:* 720
Hancock, Thomas *5:* 905
Handguns *2:* 273
Hanway, Jonas *6:* 1115
Hard disk *2:* 303
Hard drive *2:* 305
Harder, Delmar S. *2:* 333
Harding, Warren G. *5:* 875
Hardy, Godfrey Harold *5:* 855
Hardy-Weinberg equilibrium *5:* 855
Harington, Sir John *6:* 1072
Harmine *3:* 522
Harpoon *3:* **524-525**
Harrington, George F. *2:* 340
Harrington, Joseph *2:* 307
Harris, Geoffrey *3:* 553
Harris, John *6:* 1074
Harrison, Michael *5:* 860
Harrison, Ross Granville *4:* 734
Harris, Rollin *2:* 293
Hartley, Walter Noel *4:* 772
Hart, William Aaron *4:* 723

Harvard Graphics *2:* 297
Hashish *3:* 522
Hata, Sahachiro *6:* 1043
Hausdorff, Felix *6:* 1076
Hawking radiation *3:* 527
Hawking, Stephen William *3:* **526-527**
Healing *1:* 15
Health *2:* 256, 263, 269, 339, 343; *3:* 447, 468, 471, 478, 504; *4:* 673, 682, 687; *5:* 805
Hearing *1:* 12
Hearing aids and implants *3:* **528-529**; *4:* 697
Hearing impairment *2:* 315; *5:* 921
Heart *2:* 256
Heart defects, congenital *3:* 530
Heart disease *2:* 269, 382
Heart-lung machine *3:* **529-530**
Heat *1:* 27; *2:* 385; *3:* 526; *4:* 688
Heat and thermodynamics *1:* 3; *3:* **530-532**; *5:* 924
Heating *3:* **532-535**
Heat pump *3:* 535
Heat-resistant glass *6:* 1055
Heezen, Bruce Charles *4:* 704
Heezen-Ewing theory *4:* 704
Heinlein, Robert A. *6:* 1143
Heisenberg, Werner *5:* 865, 866, 889
Helicopter *1:* 33, 36; *3:* 503, **535-537**; *6:* 1078
Heliocentric theory *5:* 838
Heliography *5:* 832
Helium *2:* 330; *3:* **537-539**, 599; *4:* 637, 726; *5:* 866, 883; *6:* 1033, 1159
Helmont, Jan Baptista van *3:* 569
Hemley, R. J. *3:* 566
Hemophilia *3:* 497, 539-541; *5:* 920
Hench, Philip *1:* 14; *3:* 552
Henie, Sonja *3:* 573
Henry, Edward R. *3:* 461
Henry, Prince of Portugal *2:* 291
Hepatitis *1:* 15; *3:* **541-542**, 584

Heredity *2:* 269, 333, 404; *3:* 493, 498, 499, 522, 539, **543-547**; *4:* 688
Heroin *3:* **547**; *4:* 713
Hero of Alexandria *4:* 653; *5:* 900
Herpes *2:* 263; *3:* 542, 584
Herschel, William *3:* 461; *4:* 677, 728; *5:* 913; *6:* 1054, 1118, 1119
Hershey Chocolate Company *2:* 267
Hershey, Milton S. *2:* 267
Hertz *1:* 45; *2:* 385
Hertz, Heinrich Rudolph *2:* 388; *3:* 590; *4:* 655; *5:* 829
Hess, Harry Hammond *2:* 321; *4:* 705
Hess, Victor Franz *6:* 1163
Hevelius, Johann *4:* 710
Hevesy, György *3:* 594
Hewish, Antony *5:* 863
Hieroglyphics *1:* 41
Higgs particle *5:* 810
High-definition television (HDTV) *2:* 227; *3:* 459; *6:* 1060
High Energy Astrophysical Observatories (HEAO) *3:* 488; *6:* 1005
High-pressure physics *3:* **547-548**
High risk behavior *1:* 20
High-speed flash photography *3:* **548-549**
Highways *2:* 329
Hildebrand, Alan *2:* 329
Hilyer, Andrew Franklin *3:* 535
Hindenburg *1:* 33
Hindu-Arabic numerals *5:* 905
Hinton, William A. *6:* 1043
Hippocrates *4:* 717
Histamine *1:* 39
Histology *6:* 1069, 1070
Hitchings, George *2:* 263
Hitler, Adolf *1:* 6
H.L. *Hunley* *6:* 1078
H.M.S. *Challenger* *4:* 757
Hockey *3:* 572
Hodge, P. R. *3:* 464
Hodgkin, Dorothy Crowfoot *5:* 817; *6:* 1162

Boldfaced numbers indicate main entry pages; italicized numbers indicate volume number

Boldfaced numbers indicate main entry pages; italicized numbers indicate volume number

Boldfaced numbers indicate main entry pages; italicized numbers indicate volume number

Muscular dystrophy *4:* **717-718**; *5:* 920
Music *4:* 668
Musical instrument *5:* 897
Musical instrument, electric *4:* **718-720**
Musket *4:* 679
Mustard gas *2:* 262
Mutagen *4:* 720
Mutagenesis *4:* 720
Mutation *3:* 545; *4:* **720-722**
Muybridge, Eadweard *4:* 713, 716
MYCIN *2:* 405
Myers, Ronald *6:* 1008
Mylar *6:* 991
Myopia *2:* 407, 410; *5:* 872

N

Nabisco *2:* 356
Napier, John *2:* 339; *4:* 660
Napoleon *6:* 1172
National Advisory Committee for Aeronautics (NACA) *6:* 1156
National Aeronautics and Space Administration (NASA) *3:* 488; *5:* 941; *6:* 981, 1005
National Cancer Institute *4:* 674
National Cash Register Company *2:* 254
National Institute of Drycleaning *2:* 358
National Institutes of Health Recombinant DNA Advisory Committee *3:* 496
National Manufacturing Company *2:* 254
National Radio Astronomy Observatory (NRAO) *5:* 881
National Television System Committee (NTSC) *6:* 1060
Native Americans *5:* 922
Natta, Giulio *5:* 843
Natural gas *2:* 238; *3:* 561; *4:* 694, **723-725**, 726; *5:* 822
Natural selection *2:* 403; *3:* 544; *4:* 722; *5:* 855

The Nature of the Chemical Bond 5: 811
Nautilus 2: 292; *6:* 1026
Navigation *2:* 275, 291
Navigational satellite *4:* 704, **725-726**; *6:* 1055
Neanderthals *3:* 558
Nearsightedness *2:* 407, 410
Nebula *5:* 868; *6:* 1012, 1033, 1112
Nei Ching *1:* 16
Neisser, Albert *6:* 1043
Nelmes, Sarah *3:* 577
Neon *3:* 538; *4:* **726-727**; *5:* 883; *6:* 1033, 1159
Neon light *4:* **727-728**
Neopangaea *5:* 843
Neosalvarsan *6:* 1044
Neptune *4:* 695, **728-729**, 730; *5:* 845, 946
Neptunium *4:* **729-730**
Nero *2:* 410
Nerve fibers *4:* 733; *6:* 1039
Nerve growth factor *4:* **730-731**
Nervous system *1:* 4; *4:* 685, **731-733**; *5:* 813, 849, 914, 939; *6:* 1064
Nesmith, Bette Graham *6:* 1104
Nestlé *2:* 267
NetWare *2:* 297
Neumann, John von *3:* 485; *4:* 665
Neurology *1:* 6; *4:* 718
Neuron theory *1:* 4; *3:* 570; *4:* **733-734**; *6:* 1039
Neurotransmitter *1:* 5
Neutron *3:* 566; *4:* **734-735**; *5:* 862, 863; *6:* 1118, 1022, 1090
Neutron bomb *4:* **736-737**
Neutron star *5:* 863, 879; *6:* 1164
Newcomb, Simon *5:* 845
Newcomen, Thomas *6:* 1017
New England Digital Synclavier *6:* 1041
Newland, J. A. R. *5:* 819
Newton, Isaac *2:* 281, 283, 375; *3:* 512, 526; *4:* 647, 653, **737-739**; *5:* 840, 867; *6:* 1006, 1032, 1054
Niacin *4:* **739-740**

Nichols, Larry D. *5:* 907
Nicholson, Seth Barnes *6:* 1128
Nickel *2:* 245, 368; *4:* 692
Niemann, Albert *2:* 277
Niépce, Joseph Nicéphore *5:* 831
Nightingale, Florence *3:* 577
Niña, La 4: 693; *6:* 1148
Niño, El 4: 693
Nintendo *6:* 1130
Niobium *6:* 1068
Nipkow, Paul *6:* 1056
Nippon Electric Corporation *2:* 316
Nissen, George *6:* 1085
Nitric acid *1:* 7; *4:* **740-741**, 744, 766; *5:* 845
Nitrogen *2:* 330, 339; *3:* 514, 590; *4:* 637, 656, **741-744**, 758; *5:* 887, 914, 949; *6:* 1033, 1090
Nitrogen oxide *1:* 10
Nitroglycerin *2:* 359
Nitrous oxide *3:* 445; *4:* 744
Nobel, Alfred *2:* 359
Nobel, Ludwig *2:* 249
Nobel Prizes *1:* 6; *2:* 359, 375; *5:* 813; *6:* 1094, 1100
Nobel's Safety Powder *2:* 361
Noble gases *5:* 820
Noise reduction system *4:* **744-745**; *6:* 1019
Nollette, Abbé Jean Antoine *4:* 766
No More War! 5: 812
Non-sinusoidal *4:* 765
Non-verbal communication *5:* 921
Norman, Robert *2:* 292
Northern Lights *3:* 588
Nova *5:* 863
Nova and supernova *4:* **745-747**
Novell Inc. *2:* 295
Novocain *2:* 278; *4:* **747**
Nowcasting *6:* 1146
Nuclear fission *2:* 376, 377; *4:* 730, **748-749**, 751; *6:* 1118
Nuclear fusion *3:* 567; *4:* **749-751**; *5:* 841; *6:* 1032
Nuclear magnetic resonance (NMR) *4:* **751-753**

Boldfaced numbers indicate main entry pages; italicized numbers indicate volume number

Boldfaced numbers indicate main entry pages; italicized numbers indicate volume number

Boldfaced numbers indicate main entry pages; italicized numbers indicate volume number

Boldfaced numbers indicate main entry pages; italicized numbers indicate volume number

Thorium 5: 883
3-D 3: 549
3-D motion picture 4: 715; 6: **1065-1066**
Thunderstorm 6: 1020
Thurber, Charles 6: 1101
Thyroxine 3: 552; 6: 1094
Tides 4: 758
Time 2: 271
Time-space continuum 2: 375
Time zone 2: 273; 6: **1066-1067**
Tin 1: 40; 3: 470, 565; 4: 645, 684; 6: **1068,** 1088
Tin foil 2: 341
Tire, radial 4: 633
Tissue 1: 24; 2: 263; 3: 447, 451; 4: 731, 743, 752; 5: 914; 6: **1069-1070**
Titania 6: 1119
Titanic 5: 949
Titanium 4: 712; 6: **1070-1071**
TNT 4: 741
Toaster 6: **1071**
Toilet 6: **1072-1073**
Toll House cookies 2: 267
Tombaugh, Clyde 5: 846
Tom Thumb 6: 1081
Toothbrush and toothpaste 2: 326; 3: 460, 469; 6: **1074-1075**
Tooth decay 3: 468
Tooth extraction 3: 443
Toothpaste 3: 469
Topology 6: **1075-1077**
Tornadoes 6: 1021
Torpedo 6: 1026, **1077-1078**
Torque 3: 535
Torricelli, Evangelista 4: 684; 6: 1148
Toshiba 6: 1131
Total internal reflection 4: 652
Toys 3: 467, 479, 554; 4: 633, 635; 5: 907, 927, 929, 934; 6: 1085
Tracers 3: 594
Trachoma 2: 409
Tracked Air-Cushion Vehicles 6: 1084
Traction 3: 479
Tractor 2: 398
Traffic accidents 1: 26
Traffic signal 6: **1079**

Train and railroad 3: 453; 5: 895; 6: 1028, 1066, **1080-1085,** 1099
Training 2: 312
Trait 2: 271, 353; 3: 493
Trampoline 6: **1085-1086,** 1127
Tranquilizer (antipsychotic type) 3: 570; 6: **1086-1088**
Transducer 6: 1107
Transformer 1: 45
Transfusion 1: 23
Transistor 2: 300; 3: 528; 4: 647, 672, 697; 5: 805
Transit 6: 1128
Transmission hologram 3: 551
Transmutation of elements 6: **1088-1090**
Transplant, surgical 6: **1090-1094**
Transportation 2: 231, 250, 391, 394, 396; 3: 491, 563
Transuranium 6: 1090
Transverse waves 4: 650
Travers, Morris 4: 637; 6: 1159
Trefouel, Jacques 6: 1031
Trefouel, Thérèse 6: 1031
Tremors 2: 371
Trendar 3: 572
Treponema pallidum 6: 1043
Trevithick, Richard 6: 1080
TRH (thyrotropin-releasing hormone) 6: **1094**
Troposphere 4: 692
Truck 2: 398
Trudeau, Garry 2: 286
Truth 4: 649
Trypanosomiasis 5: 933
Tryparsamide 5: 934
Tryptophan 4: 740
Tsetse fly 5: 933
Tsiolkovsky, Konstantin 5: 902, 941
Tsunamis 2: 366
Tuberculosis 1: 20; 3: 505; 4: 682
Tumors 6: 1094
Tungsten 6: **1095,** 1153
Tungstic acid 6: 1095
Tunnel 3: 451; 6: 1030, **1095-1099**
Tunneling 6: **1099-1100**

Tuohy 2: 412
Tupper, Earl 6: 1100
Tupperware 6: **1100-1101**
Turboprop 3: 595
Turing, Alan 1: 38; 2: 228
Turpentine 5: 905
Turtle 6: 1024
Twain, Mark 6: 1103
Twins 2: 275
Tympanic membrane 1: 12
Typewriter 6: 1051, **1101-1104**
Typhoon 6: 1021
Typing correction fluid 6: **1104-1105**

U

UHF 2: 385
Uhlenbeck, George 5: 810
Ultrasonic emulsification 6: 1108
Ultrasonics 6: 1145
Ultrasonic wave 6: **1107-1108**
Ultrasonography 6: 1109
Ultrasound device 6: **1108-1110**
Ultrasound imaging 5: 860
Ultraviolet 6: 1111
Ultraviolet astronomy 6: **1111-1112**
Ultraviolet radiation 2: 282; 3: 468, 515; 4: 771, 773; 5: 827; 6: 1003, **1112-1114,** 1163
Ultraviolet radiation lamps 6: 1112, 1160
Umbrella 6: **1114-1115**
Umbria 6: 1119
Uncertainty principle 5: 865
Unconditioned reflex 5: 813
Underwater photography 6: **1115-1116**
Uniformitarianism 6: **1116-1117**
UNIVAC 2: 303; 4: 666
Universe 3: 526
University of California at Berkeley 5: 917
University of Zürich 2: 375
Unprotected sex 1: 23
Upatnieks, Juris 3: 551
Updrafts 6: 1021

Boldfaced numbers indicate main entry pages; italicized numbers indicate volume number

E u r e k a !

439

Boldfaced numbers indicate main entry pages; italicized numbers indicate volume number